To Trust

MICH.

Also by Michael Mayne:

A Year Lost and Found
Learning to Dance
Pray, Love, Remember
The Enduring Melody
This Sunrise of Wonder

To Trust and to Love

Sermons and Addresses

MICHAEL MAYNE

Edited by
JOEL W. HUFFSTETLER

DARTON · LONGMAN + TODD

In memory of George Connor,
who introduced me to the work of Michael
Mayne

First published in 2010 by
Darton, Longman and Todd Ltd
1 Spencer Court
140–142 Wandsworth High Street
London SW18 4JJ

Reprinted 2013

ISBN 978-0-232-52798-8

A catalogue record for this book is available from the British Library.

Phototypeset by Kerrypress Ltd, Luton, Bedfordshire
Printed and bound in Great Britain by Page Bros, Norwich, Norfolk

Contents

CONTENTS

vii

Acknowledgements

As this volume goes to print special thanks are due to Alison Mayne, who has given this project her blessing and her wonderfully gracious support from the very beginning. Alison gathered her husband's papers, has engaged in numerous conversations with me regarding the details of this project, and even drove my wife Debbie and me to Cuddesdon! Simply put, this collection would not exist without her.

Thanks to Brendan Walsh, Editorial Director at Darton, Longman and Todd. Brendan was Michael Mayne's editor at DLT, and he has been supportive of this project at every stage.

Thanks to the people of St. Luke's Episcopal Church in Cleveland, Tennessee. This volume was edited during the sabbatical they very lovingly and generously provided during the summer of 2009.

And special thanks to my wife, Debbie, who has been involved in and helpful with this project from day one. She has contributed to the editing of this volume in more ways than can be numbered. Thank you, my love.

Foreword by Eamon Duffy

At one level, Michael Mayne's story is the story of golden success. He was hugely gifted, blessed not only with exceptional intelligence and sensitivity, but with striking good looks, fine bones, large expressive eyes, a resonant and beautiful voice. He was a talented actor, who might have made a name on the stage if he had not opted for the priesthood. And his CV looked from the outside like the effortless trajectory of the natural establishment man – public school, Cambridge, chaplaincy to the most flamboyant bishop in the Church of England, a spell at the BBC as Head of Religious Programmes (Radio), and a succession of successful parish ministries, including a great University Church, then still packing student crowds in on Sunday evenings, drawn by a succession of celebrity speakers on topics of the moment. And, finally, Dean of Westminster, custodian of the national shrine, official organiser of Establishment big do's, a platform – I almost said a stage – on which all Michael's talents, from the pastoral to the thespian, could find what seemed their predestined outlet.

But there was more to him than that, far more. He and I arrived back in Cambridge in the same year, 1979, and I got to know him because my wife was a member of this congregation. So I was able to see at first hand what a remarkable pastor he was (*pastor* was one of his favourite words): warm and welcoming even to comparative outsiders like myself, a memorable preacher, a compassionate listener, a gracious and commanding presence in worship, with a prayerful dignity which was never self-advertising, but helped others, including me, to pray.

He and I became friends, and in the exchanges of friendship I learned something of what lay below all that. The pain of his early life: his father's suicide when Michael was only three, the poverty and instability into which he and his mother were plunged, and the special stresses of the intense, loving, but often fraught, relationship of a struggling mother and her only son.

Here, in events about which he was eventually able to speak openly in two of the addresses printed in this book, lay the key to Michael's strengths and weaknesses. He never really got over the loss of the father he could hardly remember. That first loss and all that flowed from it had left in this man, so talented, so blessed in his marriage, so poised and apparently so at home with the great and the good, a core of vulnerability and anxious unease which drove him to perfectionism. Both the anxiety and the perfectionism could be troublesome, to himself and to others – a relaxed meal with Michael might well turn into an angst-laden brain-storming session to help him decide whom to invite to Great St Mary's to draw the crowds over the coming year.

The anxieties and stresses of those Cambridge years by his own account nearly killed him. But if they could invade his peace, those inner anxieties also made him acutely sensitive to the vulnerability of others. For Michael, the understanding and acknowledgement of our own woundedness was the first step towards compassion, and often the means of unlocking the frozen feelings of others. That perception underpinned his whole understanding of ministry, and it made him a quite remarkable listener, intense, attentive, insightful, He listened, in fact, as he prayed, and it made him a skilled navigator in the sea of suffering and insecurity on which we are all to some extent travellers.

And it was suffering which fully revealed his depths as a man and a priest. Towards the end of his time in Cambridge, he fell ill with ME. It was an appalling and debilitating disease, draining him of energy and joy, and especially humiliating to a sensitive man because doctors didn't fully understand it, and people were often dismissive of what was sometimes labelled 'yuppie flu'. Struggling to come to terms with it, he decided to write it all down. The result was an intensely moving book, *A Year Lost and Found*, published after he had moved to the Abbey. It had a quite remarkable effect. Dozens, hundreds of people wrote to him, finding in his carefully crafted, but painfully honest writing, recognition, consolation and help in their own struggles with illness.

Michael knew the lonely truth about what it was to be man better than most. During his time at the Abbey he tried to make sure that a tourist venue which was always in danger of becoming a frenetic showplace, remained a sanctuary where the human spirit could be nourished and healed, through the life of prayer and the Eucharist. And he produced a series of beautiful books, distilled from his love of literature and art, and filled with wisdom and humanity born out of his own first-hand knowledge of the woundedness of the human spirit. The books conveyed the man – sensitive, widely read, self-deprecatingly humorous, filled with celebration, as well as, underneath it all, the acknowledgement of pain: *This Sunrise of Wonder*, a series of letters to his grandchildren in which he tried to pass on his own deepest resources, *Pray, Love, Remember*, a meditation on the meaning of the Abbey, and *Learning to Dance*, dedicated to Alison, his beloved wife and partner in the dance of life.

But the best and worst was to come. In retirement, planning a final book on old age and preparation for death, he was stricken down with cancer of the jaw, and that final book, *The Enduring Melody*, turned into a harrowing chronicle of hope and endurance in the face of indignity and very great suffering. It's impossible to read it without tears, and it is his best book. It brings home like nothing else I have read the traumatic human cost of much of what we call healing, and the progress of a disease devastating for so fastidious a man. Yet it's also a book full of loving attention to the small details of the natural world, full of gratitude to his family for their love and support, and it confronts with characteristic honesty his fears and sufferings, and the difficulty even for a believer in such extremity of transmitting the affirmations of faith from head to heart. Above all, it's shaped by the strength he drew from the church's daily routine of worship, especially the words of the psalms. It is a magnificent lesson in how a Christian dies, and no priest could leave a better testament. Here he is, at the end of the book.

> Twice in my life this has happened to me. I have been knocked flat, trapped by illness and wonderfully diminished. But that reality conjures up ... the great redeeming truth ... of the wounded healer ... the one made incarnate and laid low, sharing our vulnerability, our encounter with mystery, our Job-like search for answers ... And in his light, we are helped to see light: and to endure.

Looking back in 2002 on forty years of life as a priest, Michael Mayne summed up his life's ambitions: 'to be a useful pastor, and to retain my humanity'. The beautiful, honest and deceptively simple sermons and addresses collected in this book are eloquent testimony that he abundantly achieved both those ambitions.

Preface

In 2009 I wrote a thesis on Michael Mayne's five major books in completion of the Master of Sacred Theology degree at the School of Theology, the University of the South (Sewanee). The thesis is titled, "A Critical Analysis of the Writings of Michael Mayne." A revised version of the thesis is published as *Gratitude and Grace: The Writings of Michael Mayne*. While doing the research for the thesis I was made aware of the existence of hundreds of pages of Michael Mayne's unpublished sermons, addresses, lectures, and parish newsletter articles. A representative selection of these previously unpublished pieces appears in this collection.

Michael Mayne's five major books: *A Year Lost and Found* (1987, reissued in 2007); *This Sunrise of Wonder* (1995, reissued in 2008); *Pray, Love, Remember* (1998); *Learning to Dance* (2001); and *The Enduring Melody* (2006), have been well received by grateful readers the world over. The contents of *To Trust and to Love: Sermons and Addresses* provide a significant addition to his body of published work. Part I consists of sermons and addresses that follow the Christian year. Part II offers a miscellany of Mayne's sermons and addresses that are representative of the best of his ministry as a parish priest, guest preacher, and retreat leader.

To read through Michael Mayne's papers has been a great privilege, and to be able to offer more of his work to readers is a source of deep joy.

The royalties from this volume are donated to the Medical Foundation for the Care of Victims of Torture in memory of Michael Mayne.

Joel W. Huffstetler
Ripon College Cuddesdon
July 2009

Introduction

On the news that Michael Mayne had died of cancer of the jaw in October 2006, nearly every major newspaper in the United Kingdom carried an obituary. His obituarists agreed that he had been one of the most hard working and effective priests of his generation, and that by the end of his life he had come to be recognised as one of the finest writers on Christian spirituality of his time. Michael Mayne penned five major books, the first published in 1987, and the last in 2006 just weeks before his death. In the books, Mayne encourages his readers to come to experience a life marked by joy and gratitude, and an awareness of God's abiding presence and boundless love. At the same time, Mayne acknowledges in his writings the very real pain and suffering that are ever-present in the world. His books are characterised by an unflinching honesty regarding the challenges of the spiritual life, as well as its rewards. All five of Michael Mayne's major works remain in print and continue to find appreciative readers.

Michael Clement Otway Mayne was ordained in 1957 and served the church for the duration of his life. His career included time as a parish priest, diocesan staff member, broadcasting executive, and, finally, Dean of Westminster for ten years. Beginning in 1996, Mayne's 'retirement' was filled with requests to preach, speak, lead retreats, and to serve as a spiritual director.

To Trust and to Love is a representative collection of Dean Mayne's previously unpublished sermons, addresses, and newsletter articles. His papers contain no material predating his tenure as vicar of Great St Mary's (the University Church),

Cambridge, but dating from 1979 through to 2004 there are sermons, addresses, newsletter articles, meditations, and lectures totalling thousands of pages. While Dean of Westminster and then also in retirement, Mayne was a frequent guest preacher and speaker in the United Kingdom as well as in the United States.

There are those who reckon Michael Mayne to have been the finest preacher or speaker they ever heard. His sermons and writings are erudite. Mayne was a craftsman of both the spoken and the written word. At the same time, his sermons and addresses are unfailingly accessible. His work seeks not to impress, but to inspire. Martin Luther employed the phrase, 'to console and to enliven.' Mayne appropriates this phrase in expressing his own understanding of pastoral ministry. For Mayne, the pastor's vocation is to console, and to enliven those in his or her pastoral care. He writes regarding the ministry of preaching:

> Preaching demands three things of you: that you are true to the gospel; that you are true to yourself; and that you try to speak of God and the redemptive power of his love and forgiveness in terms that people understand. Implicit in that gospel is the New Testament vision of a new ordering of society, and you must also try to communicate in terms which relate to the moral, social and political concerns of your time. Sometimes it can seem an awesome task.
> (*Great St Mary's* [the University Church] *Newsletter*,
> September 1980)

Mayne approached the task of preaching with passion, and with considerable skill.

Dean Mayne was clear in his own mind that he was not an academic theologian, nor was he an original thinker in matters of theology. He was, instead, a pastor. He observes in an address included in this collection:

I do not believe there is a lovelier word than 'pastor',
nor a more important aspect of ministry than pastoral
care; and I rejoice to be part of a church that
recognizes the right of every person in every parish to
look to their clergy for care and affirmation in all the
unpredictability of their daily lives.

Mayne holds both in his published as well as his heretofore
unpublished work that the two most important lessons to
learn in life are how to trust, and how to love. He spent his
lifetime of ministry helping those in his pastoral care to learn
these two most crucial of lessons, as he himself continually
sought to learn them. Mayne clearly understood that he too
was a pilgrim, not one who had arrived.

To trust, and to love. The contents of this collection reflect
Michael Mayne's faith in God whose presence can be trusted,
and whose nature is love.

Chronology

Michael Clement Otway Mayne
Born 10 September 1929, Harlestone, Northamptonshire

1933	London
1939	Torbay
1942 – 49	King's School, Canterbury
1949 – 51	National Service, Royal Air Force
1951 – 55	Corpus Christi College, Cambridge
1955 – 57	Cuddesdon Theological College
1957 – 59	Curate, St John's, Harpenden (Diocese of St Albans)
1959 – 65	Domestic Chaplain to Mervyn Stockwood, Bishop of Southwark 16 October 1965 – Married Alison McKie in Southwark Cathedral
1965 – 72	Vicar St George's, Norton, Letchworth (Diocese of St Albans)
1972 – 79	Head of Religious Programmes, BBC Radio (lived in Harpenden)
1979 – 86	Vicar of Great St Mary's (the University Church), Cambridge (Diocese of Ely)
1986 – 96	Dean of Westminster
1996 – 2006	Retirement in Salisbury

Died 22 October 2006

Part one

Through the Christian Year

1

A Wondering Silence

ADVENT 1998

St Thomas's Church, Salisbury

I can remember, when I was about six or seven, lying in bed in the dark and wondering about the sheer size of things, and what God looked like, and trying to imagine how things could go on for ever and ever; and wondering too, when people died, as my father had, just what happened to them. And I was told that I would understand better when I was grown up; but I didn't and I don't. Oh, I know about a million things I didn't know about then, like birds and music and the plays of Shakespeare and sickness and being in love, but as for what happens when we die, and what God looks like and what heaven may be like – well, even Shakespeare didn't know that. He spoke of 'the mystery of things'. And they remain a mystery; the windows of heaven are closed and we're all left like children wondering what it's like, out there in the dark.

And yet it's not quite that simple. Nothing ever is. At this time of year many children will have an Advent calendar, with their 24 little closed windows. You're supposed to open them one at a time, but most children take a peek or two ahead. For anything may lie behind those windows and you've no idea whether it's going to be a star or a candle or a donkey, or even in these secular days a Teletubby or a Big Mac or even Bart Simpson. Yet the final window is always the same. The final window, which you open on Christmas Eve, is always a picture of Mary and Joseph and the baby lying in

3

the manger. The one who grows up to become for Christians the only accurate window into God.

And our lives feel a bit like these Advent calendars. You never know what's coming next, as one by one the windows of your life are pulled open to reveal the unpredictable: the man or woman we're going to marry. A new job, a new home, a new baby. Or an illness; or the death of someone we love. One by one the windows open, and they illuminate or darken our lives and create our particular story. Yet the last window, the window that would show us what lies the other side of death, remains tight shut, and when our time comes we pass through death's door into darkness, reduced once again to the state of children wondering what may lie out there in the dark.

Or so it has seemed to men and women down the centuries. But Christians tell a different story. We don't deny the mystery. We can't guess at the life of heaven or the nature of the final judgment. And yet, because of what lies behind that final window in the Advent calendar, we see the darkness in a different light. We see it in the light of what we call the Incarnation, in the light of this child's birth and life and death and resurrection. God, in every sense, giving us his Word. His Word made flesh in Jesus, whom John the Baptist recognised as the promised Messiah, at once the proclaimer of God's Kingdom and the window into God.

He's a disturbing figure, John, standing in the desert like some roughly-dressed hermit and quoting Isaiah, that prophet who 700 years earlier had spoken words of comfort to the Jewish refugees exiled in Babylon and given them a vision of a new and restored creation. Isaiah who had spoken of another prophet who would come to be a voice crying in the wilderness. And John the Baptiser says: 'I am that voice' as he urges the people to repent and so be ready for the God who is about to reveal his Word in a dramatically new and decisive way.

4

I have a friend, an American novelist [Frederick Buechner], who likens God to a poet searching for exactly the right word:

> (God) tries Noah, but Noah is a drinking man, and (he) tries Abraham, but Abraham is a little too Mesopotamian with all those wives and whiskers. Tries Moses, but Moses himself is trying too hard; and David too handsome for his own good ... Tries John the Baptist with his locusts and honey, who might almost have worked except for something small but crucial like a sense of the ridiculous or a balanced diet. Word after word God tries ... and then he finally tries ... to get ... into one final Word what he is and what human is and why the suffering of love is precious and how the peace of God is a tiger in the blood. And the Word that God finds is this one, Jesus of Nazareth, all of it coming alive finally in this life, the Word finally made flesh in this flesh ...

Many people think that the Christian faith is basically saying: 'Do this!' or 'Don't do that!' It isn't. It's saying: 'Look! Pay attention! Look at God and his creation and each other with changed eyes because of what you see in Christ.' Those who seek to communicate the Christian faith should be (like John the Baptist) saying: 'Don't look at me – look at him. Listen to his word as he speaks of the Mystery, for he alone of all our human race saw into the heart of God and said that his name is Father and his nature Love.' It's what artists do. An artist is one who takes us by the arm and says: 'Let me show you what things look like to me. See how even the unlikeliest object is transformed when the light falls upon it in a certain way.' So John the Baptist looks at Jesus of Nazareth and says: 'Look closely at this man who comes to me to be baptised and you will see his glory.' And what the Christian faith says is: 'Come and see what life and death look like, in the light of Christ, so that you may learn not to fear them. And come and see what

God looks like, and what the world looks like, and what every man, woman and child looks like, in the light of Christ so that you may learn to love them. He is not only the window into what God is like, but into what it means to be human'.

But there is one detail in which John the Baptist was both right and wrong. And it is a detail that changes everything. I said that he looked at Jesus and saw his glory. 'There stands one among you', he said, 'the straps of whose sandals I am not worthy to unloose'. Whenever I hear those words my mind goes to that scene three years later in an upper room. For there I see Jesus turn all acknowledged religious and social protocol on their head by stooping and kneeling on the dusty floor in order to undo the straps of his friends' sandals and begin to wash their dusty feet. And the word 'glory' must be rethought and newly defined.

For consider. That was the most menial service performed by a slave, one who had no status and no rights. John the Baptist could think of no more powerful way of comparing his own insignificance with the greatness of God's Messiah. Yet Jesus, by that last startling action on Maundy Thursday, showed how in him the majesty and compassion of God are mysteriously combined. It would have astonished John. It astonished the disciples. Yet it is in fact the defining moment when we understand that in Jesus Christ the two aspects of God – his majesty and his love – are most wonderfully combined.

If the birth of a baby in a stable and the tortured body of a man hanging on a cross are the two most revealing windows into God, the unstrapping of sandals and the washing of dusty feet is no less powerful a disclosure. For here is a God who shows the nature of his power and majesty by humbly kneeling at our feet. For that kind of practical service is how love always responds to human need. And it is that proper love, that Christlike love, which – as we begin to prepare for Christmas – should reduce us to a wondering silence; and by which we shall one day be judged.

6

The Silence of Our Full Attention

CHRISTMAS EVE DAY 1989

St Margaret's Church, Westminster

The final words of the Epistle from Zechariah: 'Be silent, all flesh, before the Lord; for he has roused himself from his holy dwelling.'

Many clergy have recurring dreams.

This dream, for me, takes two forms. In the first I am standing at the altar celebrating the Eucharist but I simply cannot find the right page. Every page in the book is either blank or in Japanese.

In the second dream I am standing in the pulpit just like this about to preach a sermon and I open and shut my mouth but nothing emerges, for I am speechless and ill-prepared and have nothing to say.

This morning I thought that dream might come true. For it has been a busy week, one of those weeks when you go from event to event. What little time I have had to think has gone in preparing two Christmas sermons: one for tonight's Midnight Eucharist; the other for the Abbey Eucharist tomorrow. But there, lurking in the shadows was the Sunday of Christmas Eve: neither one thing nor another, hardly Advent, not yet Christmas: a Sunday-shaped blank, somehow to be filled with the right words.

And then I saw that as a small parable.

For it is precisely here, where we stand speechless and over-pressed and uninspired and empty that God acts. And it is not in any words of ours, but only in silence and in stillness that we shall catch the song of the angels and be truly brought face to face with the Word made flesh.

'Be silent, all flesh, before the Lord; for he has roused himself from his holy dwelling.' 'A virgin shall conceive and bear a son, and his name shall be called Emmanuel, which means, God with us.'

Tonight this church and our Abbey and a million churches all over the world will be full to the doors to celebrate that most ordinary and extraordinary of events: the birth of a child. God acts once in history in a way so simple, so direct, so startling, that we are stopped short in our tracks. Here is an event which changes everything; an event utterly unexpected and utterly undeserved: a baby in a wooden manger who by the time he hangs on his wooden cross will have so illuminated the nature of God that it is as if a great blazing sun has been set in the world to light our way and warm our hearts.

But what a mystery it is! That God – the mysterious, unimaginable maker of all things – should make himself known in the only terms we could understand, make himself known as love, and in Jesus speak to our lives at their deepest point. His name is Emmanuel, God with us. Only in silence, the silence of our full attention, can such a truth begin to be heard. And silence, the silence of wondering love, is the only adequate response. Or music, perhaps. Silence or music.

What need of words, then, as Christmas draws so close? Except those words of warning that cut through our talkative lives and say 'be still!' 'Be silent, all flesh, before the Lord!' Stop your busy-ness. Give attention to God and what he is telling you of himself. He would have us know that he is Christ–like. He would have our full attention this Christmas that we may stop thinking of the past, or worrying about the future, and give this the present wholly to his love by being faithful to his grace in Jesus Christ.

The Gift of a Saviour

CHRISTMAS EVE MIDNIGHT EUCHARIST 1989

Westminster Abbey

Tonight you have come through the dark streets into the subdued lights and the stillness of this ancient Abbey on what is the most breathtaking night in the year.

Here for nearly a thousand years men and women, little different from us in their hopes and fears and griefs and joys, have been drawn out of the darkness of their world by the compelling power of a light which can never be quenched. The light of the child of Bethlehem, whose life and teaching and death and rising illuminate once and for all time the true nature of God in whose likeness this child shows us all to be made.

Who is this God whom we worship in all the beauty of soaring stone and colour and music? Is he not the Lord most high, whom none can set eyes on and live, immortal, invisible, One beyond our power to imagine or describe?

Yes, all that; but there is something more. For God would not be God if we could know him fully, but neither would he be God if we couldn't know him at all. And so there is 'something more'.

And the 'something more' is totally different and wholly unexpected.

The 'something more' is a baby lying in the straw.

The 'something more' is God made flesh, the Word, yet unable to speak a word. 'The maker of the stars and sea, become a child on earth for me.'

The man that child became was to say 'whoever has seen me has seen the Father'. And so the 'something more' is that God is Christlike.

Who could have imagined that God would choose to express himself in so unexpected a place and in so human a form? Yet in what other way could we know the truth about God: about his tender compassion and his grace. Only what is human speaks to us in words and actions we can understand. Here is a God who is not wholly removed from us, but a God who suffers for us and with us and who loves each one of us with a love beyond anything we can at present conceive.

In the words of St. Luke:

> 'In the tender compassion of our God the rising Sun
> has come from on high to visit us to give light to
> those who dwell in darkness and the shadow of death,
> and to guide our feet into the way of peace.'

There are times when we question how such a thing can be, this greatest of all mysteries: God made known in Christ. Times when we grapple with our faith and need to think through with our minds what we respond to with our hearts.

But I suggest to you that the dawn of Christmas Day is not one of them. For what God asks of us tonight is to stretch out our hands as trustingly as a child receiving a present at Christmas and receive from him this gift of a Saviour.

> The darkest time in the year,
> The poorest place in town,
> Cold, and a taste of fear,
> Man and woman alone.
> What can we hope for here?
> More light than we can learn,
> More wealth than we can treasure,
> More love than we can earn,
> More peace than we can measure,
> Because one child is born.

4

Now I Am One of You

CHRISTMAS DAY 1986

Westminster Abbey

'And is it true? and is it true
This most tremendous tale of all,
Seen in a stained glass window's hue,
A baby in an ox's stall?
The maker of the stars and sea
Become a child on earth for me?'

It is a fact so simple that a child can grasp it: a mother and her baby in a manger. And yet it is a mystery no words can properly capture or describe: God made man. A mystery which will only reveal itself at all to those who approach it like a child, with a childlike sense of wonder and a child's sense of trust. For what Christmas declares is this: that God makes himself known in Jesus Christ, and that he makes himself known as love.

And this morning, in every nation on earth, in great cathedrals rich with incense and colour, in village churches where this truth has been proclaimed for a thousand years, in the labour camps of Russia or the detention cells of South Africa, men and women and children are celebrating with joy the great mystery of this particular human birth.

It is indeed a strange and unlikely truth that we Christians have to give to the world. Most people would like to think there is a God, a creative power behind and within the universe, and that this power is personal and loving.

But they find it hard to relate that truth to the pain and unfairness of life. The world doesn't feel or look as if it's made by a God who is love. Yet it is exactly at that point – where what we long for and what we experience don't seem to fit or make sense – that God answers us with his Word. His Word made flesh. 'Jesus', wrote John Donne, 'contracts the immensities and focuses the infinite'.

God is not indifferent. God immerses himself in his creation and is born a man, one exactly like ourselves, and at the crib in Bethlehem the image of God as a power to be afraid of, as somehow speaking through the blind forces of nature – that image dies. We see God in human terms: not up there, somewhere far off and over against us, but here, made flesh, *for* us and *with* us and in our midst.

You may know the story of Father Damien who, a hundred years ago, went at his own request to a leper colony before there was any cure for leprosy. One day, putting his foot into water to wash it, he could no longer feel the water was hot and he knew he too had become a leper. And so he could begin his next Sunday sermon: 'Now I too am one of you'. That isn't simply an illustration of a life which was inspired by the love of God: it's also a parable of the incarnation, of the meaning of the Word made flesh. 'Now I too am one of you.' God suffers in and with his creatures. How could it be otherwise if he is Love?

'No one has ever seen God', writes St. John. 'It is the only Son, he who is nearest to the Father's heart, who has made him known.' And he has made him known in the only terms we can understand: in human terms, as the man Jesus Christ. His every word and action is radiated by his knowledge of the Father, and so we can say that God is like a man who heals the sick and loves the sinner; who takes a basin and towel and washes his disciples' feet; who, when nailed to a cross, forgives those who are nailing him there.

'Love came down at Christmas' we sing in a familiar carol; love was made flesh. And if we are tempted to say 'that's not

12

my idea of God', then the reply comes back from the pages of the New Testament 'then your idea of God must change'. For we cannot now say the word 'God' without saying the word 'Jesus', and how can we say the word 'Jesus' without saying the word 'love'?

So Christmas comes to challenge our concept of God. It's no good having some fixed idea of God and trying to make Jesus Christ fit into it. For if we really believe that in this man God was reconciling the world to himself, then we must be prepared (if need be) to have our understanding of God totally and radically changed.

It will change our idea of what God is once we see that God is best understood not in terms of the power of the blind forces of nature, but in terms of love. But it changes too our idea of what love is. For love is not soft and yielding and emotional. Love is diamond-hard and costly. Jesus defines what love is: it is a giving of yourself to others; it is a refusal to hate whatever the cost; it is a refusal to be moved from what you know in your heart to be true and good and right. Love is quite often a kind of dying.

And so Christmas changes too our idea of what man is, and the sight of this one true human being has haunted the world ever since. Christmas says 'the Saviour is born', and he *is* our Saviour because he is both what God means by man, and also (and here is a mystery which must reduce us to silence and wonder) what man means by God.

And so what does it mean to celebrate Christmas? It doesn't just mean indulging in nostalgia and escaping into an unreal world of forced goodwill, of tinsel and turkey and fairy lights. To celebrate Christmas means first and foremost to believe that God has spoken his final and definitive word in history, no matter how much clamour the world keeps up, or that the world chooses to ignore it. To celebrate Christmas is to say *Amen* in the depth of my being to the Word God has spoken in this particular birth and life and death and resurrection. If, beyond the glimmer of candles, beyond the carols and the fragrance of the Christmas tree, we can from our hearts answer 'Yes' to God's love in Jesus Christ, then Christmas really takes place and the Christ who came once at Bethlehem and took possession of the world, is born again in us and takes possession of our hearts.

5

A Christmas Message

JANUARY 1981

*Great St Mary's (the University Church, Cambridge)
Newsletter*

Christmas is hung about with memories. Memories from childhood; memories of family Christmasses, the candlelit church packed for the Midnight Eucharist; of generosity and goodwill. But memories easily distort the reality; and even the central event of Christmas, a woman having a baby in difficult conditions away from home, has been dulled and distorted by scores of Nativity plays and cribs, genteel plaster figures in the clean straw.

But Christmas cannot be so confined, for it celebrates a mystery of awful power. The mystery St John calls 'the Word made flesh': the breathtaking claim that God is like Jesus, that the Word who said 'Let there be light' and there was light, and who named each living creature, should be content to be a child learning his first halting words at his mother's knee.

Christmas, like Easter, allows us to see once in time what is eternal and unchanging. We cannot take in the reality of Love at the heart of things except in simple human terms: in terms of a baby, a healing action, a forgiving word, a washing of feet, a breaking of bread, a cross and an empty grave. But once our eyes are open to the fact that God is not only powerful beyond our imagining but to be found in the minute particulars of life; that he is not over against us, but one with us; that he is, in a word, Christlike; then we can never look at anything in the same way again.

Each year we celebrate because a child is born. And we are right to do so because that obscure birth, in the light of all that followed from it, was a decisive moment in history, when something totally new began. But, if we are wise, we see the wooden manger of Bethlehem transmuted into the wooden cross of Calvary, and acknowledge in our world a continuing web of suffering which has that Cross at its centre.

What God gives us in the words and actions, the dying and rising, of Christ is no magical deliverance from human pain, but a light in our darkness, the power to survive, the conviction that what we see in that baby, and the man he became, tells us more about the reality at the heart of the universe than anything else. Love of that quality is the most powerful force in the world.

Remember, then, this Christmas those who are enduring darkness: among them Jean Waddell and John and Audrey Coleman imprisoned in Iran, together with their Bishop-in-exile, Hassan Deqhani-Tafti; and pray that they and those like them may be upheld by this conviction about the reality of the love of God in Christ.

Following the Star

THE FEAST OF THE EPIPHANY 1989

Westminster Abbey

When (after some 50 years had passed) St Matthew wrote down the story of the birth of Jesus, he was writing out of his knowledge of the man that child became: what he knew of his death and (more important) what he had experienced of his Resurrection and of the Church which then spread like wild-fire across the known world. He alone of the four gospel-writers decides to tell the story of his birth, and to do so in a way which would at once alert his hearers to certain truths.

He speaks of a stable, and of some shepherds coming to a manger. By this he is saying: Here is a birth so *ordinary* that simple folk can understand and respond to it.

He then goes on to speak of a star and Wise Men from the East bringing treasures to lay at this child's feet. By this he is saying: And here is a birth so *extraordinary* that it speaks to people of all nations. This child is like a great star illuminating everyone's lives and claiming their allegiance.

This is another way of saying what in the fourth gospel Jesus says of himself: 'I am the light of the world.' 'I am the truth.' The truth about God's love. The truth about man, made in God's likeness. Until now these truths have been hidden: now in Jesus they are revealed. And this is what Epiphany means: a revealing, a shining forth.

What does it mean for us to follow the star?

In one of his finest poems, *A Christmas Oratorio*, W.H. Auden puts these words into the mouths of the three Wise

17

Men as they explain why they choose to follow the star that will lead them to Christ.

'To discover how to be *truthful* now
Is the reason I follow the star' says the first.
'To discover how to be *living* now,
Is the reason I follow the star' says the second.
'To discover how to be *loving* now,
Is the reason I follow the star' says the third.

How to be truthful: how to know the truth and follow the truth. 'You shall know the truth' said Jesus, 'and the truth will set you free.'

How to be living now: how to live to God in *this* moment, neither a slave of the past, nor anxious about the future. 'Take no thought for the morrow' said Jesus, 'trust in God and trust in me.'

How to be loving now: how to respond to other people with openness and love. 'Love God' said Jesus, 'and love your neighbour as you love yourself.'

Those are the reasons the wise follow the light which came into the world at Bethlehem. And in Auden's poem the Wise Men then speak in unison and say:

'To discover how to be *human* now
Is the reason we follow this star.'

'A human being' it has been said, 'is the creature made visible in the mirror of Jesus Christ'. In other words, Jesus shows us what God means by man: a being of mystery and wonder whose destiny is union with God. And when you look at Jesus as he reveals the true potential of our human nature we can believe it; and we can believe too that the ultimate purpose of creation is the unity of all mankind in Christ: the breaking down of oppression, the righting of wrongs, and the establishing of a new order of peace and justice on the earth.

'To discover how to be human now,
Is the reason we follow this star.'

Learning how to be human now will mean dealing with other persons with compassion and openness and love. And bringing to the God revealed in Jesus Christ our best gifts of attention and trust.

Perhaps it was put best by St Paul when he wrote that we are 'to shine like stars in a dark world'. And ever since, whenever a person is sufficiently drawn to Christ as to say 'Lord, take my heart', then there is indeed a small Epiphany, a shining forth of light in the dark.

Absurdly and Gloriously Different

THE WEEK OF PRAYER FOR CHRISTIAN UNITY 1996

Westminster Abbey

A few months ago I knelt, as others here will have done, in the great church of reconciliation on that hillside in Burgundy known as Taizé. I knelt in silence, amongst hundreds of similar figures, also kneeling or sitting on the ground. German, French and English backpackers, Polish and South African students, pilgrims from Mexico and the Ukraine and India; Orthodox and Catholics, Lutherans and Methodists, Anglicans and Baptists on their journey of faith; others still searching for a truth to live by. The old and the middle-aged, but mainly the young: all of us drawn to that hillside and held by that stillness. And finding there, each in his or her own way, the spirit of the one who alone of all our race faced the transcendent mystery and said that his name was Father and his nature love.

There are some who find a security in labelling themselves and others. They like things to be neat and tidy: not just the judgmental divide of 'I am a saved sheep, you are an unbelieving goat', but 'I am a conservative evangelical sheep who has been slain in the Spirit and you are a liberal sheep who clearly hasn't, and there's a great gulf between us.'

Yet when the Philippian gaoler asked Paul 'What must I do to be saved?' he was told 'Believe on the Lord Jesus'; not because we are then plucked out of the common herd and set apart in some exclusive way, but because in the light of Jesus

Christ the scales fall from our eyes and we are set free to be what we truly are: human beings revealed in all their true potential. Children of one heavenly Father, created by love for love, and destined for the life of the Kingdom.

But no-one ever mentioned uniformity, and we only have to look at one another with frank and loving eyes to know that God must revel in diversity. We are absurdly and gloriously different, and your approach to God is not my approach, your gifts are not my gifts, your style is not my style, and life is the richer for it. For what would seem to please God is not that we conform to some boring uniformity, but that we respond to him in what Archbishop Desmond Tutu would call the marvellous diversity of 'the rainbow people of God'.

Perhaps the essence of sin is the heresy of individualism: when I act as a self-contained unit, grateful that I am this particular and private 'me' and not 'you'. That is a heresy because it is the reversal of God's intention. Of course each of us is unique. Of course I look out at the world through my own particular eyes. Yet the very essence of being a person lies in relating to others. Only in that give-and-take, only in the recognition that each of us is special, yet all of us have so very much in common, do we break through into our full and proper humanity. Do you know that moment in the Journals of Thomas Merton when suddenly, on a particular street corner, he is overwhelmed by 'the realization that I loved all these people, that they were mine and I theirs, that we could not be alien to one another even though we were total strangers. If only everyone could realize this' he goes on, 'but it could never be explained. There is no way of telling people that they are all walking around shining like the sun'.

Such an insight into what it actually means to be a human being, enables us to see others with love, aware of the mystery of the God whose life-giving Spirit lies at the very centre of our being.

21

Now if it is true that we are properly and inevitably diverse, and if it is true that what already unites us is that we are made in the divine image, then it follows that I should not dismiss the insights of other faiths, or deny their glimpses of truth and their values where they differ from mine, but rather affirm and celebrate the truth whenever it appears. I believe I will be a better Christian not if I mindlessly refute the Jew, the Muslim, the Hindu and the Buddhist, nor if I pretend that our differences are unimportant, but if I can affirm what may be deep insights about God and about the human condition; but *go still further*. As I will be a better Anglican or Methodist or Roman Catholic, not if I refute the teaching of other traditions, but if I can recognize those distinctive, but lesser truths we each guard and value while saying 'Yes' to those greater, more powerful truths that undergird us all: our given unity in Christ. Our common baptism in him. Our belief that through his Cross and Resurrection we are redeemed and forgiven. Our desire to be open to his Holy Spirit, and our common concern for his Kingdom.

The ecumenism that is our concern is not about that final doctrinal agreement that will right the wrongs of history. It is rather about two things. The first is that kind of joint practical action that is a powerful expression of the love of God, and of which in these last years a fine example is what has come to be known as The Mersey Miracle: the joint work of Archbishop Derek Worlock, Bishop David Sheppard and the Free Church Moderator in that most sectarian of cities, Liverpool. Ask them what they have learned and they will say (and I quote): 'A quite new appreciation of the richness and diversity which every Christian tradition has to bring to the whole, and a breaking down of inherited prejudice'.

I have rarely been as moved as I was here a few years ago when on a Good Friday hundreds came in procession from Westminster Cathedral to the Abbey with a large wooden cross from Londonderry and filled the nave, and heard a Roman Catholic priest, a Church of Ireland priest and a Free

Church minister speak of their shame at the hatred and violence of Ulster and ask each other's forgiveness. Having identified ourselves with their act of penance we then sang: 'When I survey the wondrous Cross'.

And when, please God, a just and lasting peace comes to Ireland, North and South, the untold heroes will be those from both sides of the religious divide who have worked in small communities for reconciliation and forgiveness. I know of one such, just off the Shankhill Road, *Cornerstone*, a largely lay community of Roman Catholics and Protestants who, for the past twenty years, whenever there was a sectarian killing, immediately went out two by two, one from each tradition, to visit the homes of the bereaved and together attend the funeral of the victims.

And, coming nearer home, I believe that the best ecumenical action the Westminster Christian Council has taken was to set up its Homelessness Committee which has met in a little room at German Christ Church, and which recently recommended to the Council a joint Rent Deposit Scheme to help homeless young people in conjunction with Centrepoint. From such a fund it is intended to advance rents and deposits so that young people have a chance to become tenants, in addition to providing volunteers to help such young people tackle the problem of being first time tenants. Our churches were set a target of £10,000. To date we have given nearly £13,000. The only anxiety now is that the Government is proposing cutting housing benefit to people under 25, and if they do so imaginative schemes of this kind will be hit very hard.

But if our first task is to demonstrate together the love of God in joint practical social actions like this, our other task is quite different. To quote the words of a great ecumenist, Henry Chadwick: 'True ecumenism is listening and kneeling in the presence of God with brothers and sisters in Christ from whom the accidents of history divided us, and asking how we might together learn the gospel way of authentic reconciliation'. Kneeling together, as at Taizé, in the presence of God and not speaking but listening. Seeking to understand our different histories so that there may be a healing of memories. For, in the words of the black American writer Maya Angelou, 'History, despite its wrenching pain, cannot be unlived, but if faced with courage, need not be lived again.'

When the South African leader, F.W. de Klerk, was asked if it was international sanctions which finally brought about the end of apartheid he replied: 'It was not the sanctions. It was deep self-analysis on our knees before God'. In the inter-denominational language of penitence and prayer and con-templation edges blur, definitions shift, and room may be found amidst all our chatter for the amazing work of the Holy Spirit.

So I end on a note of hope. Which is not the same as cheerful but unrealistic optimism. For hope, Christian hope, is a state of mind. It is a dimension of the soul, an orientation of the heart, and it is anchored beyond our everyday horizons in the God revealed through Jesus Christ. We are what we are, as wonderfully diverse in our approach to the mystery of God as the colours of the rainbow. And yet, though at one level we remain divided, there is a deeper truth. For just as the red and yellow and green and indigo and violet stem from a single ray of light, so each tradition stems from that single source of light which is Jesus Christ. 'There *is* one Lord, one faith, one baptism' and all who believe that in Jesus we see God and put their faith in him are already one in Christ. That is what we are: it is something given, something of our essence. So let us celebrate this unity that is already ours in God's new creation, in all our rainbow-hued diversity, looking to Christ who, in the darkness of the world, is its one true source of light.

8

Lord, Have Mercy on Me, a Sinner

ASH WEDNESDAY 1991

Westminster Abbey

For me the most valid, effective and powerful prayer that can be said daily at this present time during the war in the Gulf is the prayer that is said at the heart of every Eucharist: O Lamb of God, that takest away the sins of the world, have mercy upon us. O Lamb of God, that takest away the sins of the world, grant us thy peace.

What is good about that prayer is that it starts with penitence: it echoes the words of the man on his knees in the temple, whose prayer is commended by Jesus: 'Lord, have mercy on me a sinner.'

It has been well said that instead of hating the people we think of as war-makers, we should first hate the appetites and the disorder in our own souls, which are the causes of war and violence of every kind. If I love peace, then I must hate injustice, hate tyranny, hate envy, hate greed, hate selfishness, hate aggression – but hate those things in myself, not in another.

There are many days in the Christian year which focus on the glory to which we are called: the beauty of God's Kingdom, the reality of God's love in Christ, the wonder of our being created in his likeness, the hope of what lies in store for us as we open ourselves to his Spirit and grow in his love.

But there are two particular days in the year when we are faced in a dramatic way with the fact of our sinfulness and our mortality. The first is Good Friday, when we are faced with the stark reality of the Cross and see how our words and actions so grievously wound us and other people and the God whose life is within us all. And the second day, when we are called to face the stark reality of what we are and what we do, and called upon to repent and throw ourselves upon God's mercy, is today, Ash Wednesday.

In a few minutes I shall be inviting those who wish to come to the altar rail, kneel down, and be signed on their forehead with the sign of the Cross from the ashes made from the burnt palms from last Palm Sunday. This is a very ancient custom which originated in the 6th century, when it was confined to public penitents who were doing penance for grave sins against the community, whom the clergy tried to comfort and encourage by submitting themselves to the same public humiliation. But the Church in one of her moments of wisdom very soon saw the value of such a natural yet deliberate act of penitence, and for a thousand years this has been done in the greater part of Christendom on this day.

Don't think of it as a negative action. On the contrary, it's a very positive and creative thing for us to do if we take seriously our Christian journey, and our need to grow both in self-knowledge and self-discipline, which can lead us to a greater awareness of the love and mercy of God.

If you do choose to come forward this evening for the imposition of ashes, it must be because you wish it and believe it can be of value to you at the beginning of this Lent. And as the ash is placed on your forehead the priest will say: 'Remember that you are dust, and to dust you shall return. Turn away from sin and be faithful to Christ.'

You may like to let the Cross placed on your forehead remind you of two things: a) the Cross of Jesus. In other words, what it cost God to give us our freedom, to forgive us our sins and to win us back to himself. And b), the Cross that was placed on your forehead at your baptism. In other words, the sign you were then given that the way of self-giving love by which we shall obtain union with God, is costly, for it demands of us the humility and honesty it takes to repent and to say from the heart: 'Lord, have mercy on me a sinner.'

9

Thoughts on Lent

MARCH 1981

*Great St Mary's (the University Church, Cambridge)
Newsletter*

'May I baptise you in the Holy Spirit?' asked the stranger the other morning, stopping me in Great St Mary's half-way down the aisle, and placing a heavy hand on my head. 'If you wish' I replied, rather feebly. 'I already have' he said. 'Now you are a born-again Christian.'

I told the story once or twice, and people laughed. And yet .... It was a few days later that Bishop Stephen Verney gave a powerful University Service address on repentance. He defined that much misunderstood word as a change of consciousness so that 'we begin to see things differently, and to feel and desire differently ... and to choose differently'. There are no other words for it: it is, as Jesus said to Nicodemus, like being born again. 'And for me' added Stephen Verney, 'it has to happen every day anew.'

'Born-again' Christians. We wouldn't use that language, most of us; but what about the claim it expresses, that in Christ we really are *new* creatures, seeing God and each other and the world and its affairs with new eyes? Familiarity has defused the revolutionary nature of the Gospel: its power to change us, and its power to turn the world's standards on their heads. We neither expect, nor much want, to be changed.

Lent, which is above all a time for growing (in vision and understanding) is about repentance properly understood: a changed awareness of *how things truly are* when seen in the light of God's revealing of himself in Christ. That is to say, in the light of justice, compassion and love. Repentance will change me: it will not make me grovel to a God of whom I am afraid; it will deepen my trust and my love, and allow me to be more truly myself.

But it should do much more. (And this is where we don't really want to know.) It should spur me to question widely-held assumptions within our society. It should force me to recognise my membership of the human race, to admit that in the great, divisive issues of our day (world poverty, economic and social justice, racism, nuclear defence and the 'just war', unemployment, inflation) there is a *moral* dimension, and for Christians what is *right* is once and for all defined in terms of the wholly unreasonable ethic of the Sermon on the Mount; turning the other cheek, going two miles with somebody who makes you go one, and loving your enemies.

It would be foolish to think that the application of the Christian ethic to our political and social choices as a nation is not complex in the extreme. Yet, if a good number of Christian 'fools' are not pointing, for example, to the moral case for the renunciation of nuclear arms, and reminding the world of the radical teaching of Christ, the great disturber of the peace, then we shall be rich enough in common sense but poor in vision.

Of course the readiness to apply, and attempt to live by, the teaching of Jesus, and be changed by his Spirit, is costly. For him, the decision to carry into the heart of the power structure what he believed about the quality of life led to the Cross. For many today it means persecution and imprisonment. For us, perhaps no more than the anger and derision attracted by those who say what many would rather not hear.

Lent is a time for repentance. For seeing how (in Christ's eyes) things truly are, and how they might be; for meditating on our willingness to be broken. So I shall try to use it as a time for making space in my life for a bit more silence; and for attempting to live a bit more simply. But also for trying better to understand how the Gospel relates to some of the political questions which most profoundly affect us all, and for looking again at some of my most deeply-engrained prejudices and assumptions. I hope you will consider doing the same.

10

The Astonishing Nature of God's Love

LENT 1987

Westminster Abbey

The opening words of this service, from Charles Wesley's hymn:

> O for a heart to praise my God,
> A heart from sin set free.

We read that Jesus came preaching the Gospel of repentance: 'Repent, for the Kingdom of God is at hand.' And it is clear that people heard his words with wonder and delight.

Yet for us the word 'repent' may seem a dark and threatening word, which we equate with feelings of guilt. It fails to express that life-changing experience of which the Gospels speak, in which Jesus freed people of their fear and guilt and defensiveness and they were able to find in him forgiveness and the kind of security they had never known. Perhaps the word has unhappy overtones for some of us because too many of those who have preached repentance have preached hell-fire and turned the Gospel of love into a Gospel of fear, and so have distorted the Gospel of Jesus whose constant concern was to bring men and women to a realisation of the astonishing nature of God's love for them.

And yet Charles Wesley was right. The publican in Our Lord's parable of the Pharisee and the publican with his words 'Lord, have mercy on me a sinner' was right. 'O for a heart to praise my God, a heart from sin set free' is the only honest starting-point for any of us.

For I do not think we begin to understand the damage our sin does to us and to others and often those we love. And by our *sin* I mean essentially that strange and compulsive self-love and self-concern which so diminishes the people we might be. It isn't only our words and actions which can cause suffering to others, either deliberately or thoughtlessly. It is also our lack of thought, our lack of imagination, our lack of compassion which holds us back and prevents us from those generous, encouraging and loving acts of which we are all capable because we are made in the likeness of God. And just because on the one hand few of us are notorious sinners, and on the other few of us are aware of our true potential, then we may find it easy to say the words of the general confession; but the words are surface words, and we can rarely be said to *repent*.

Now in the New Testament the word 'repent' doesn't mean taking some action which is negative and backward-looking, wringing your hands and endulging in an agony of guilt. On the contrary, repentance means looking at Jesus. It describes a shift in your understanding, a sudden recognition of an extraordinary truth: the truth of God's unconditional love for you. Repentance is my instinctive response to the discovery that I am loved by God in a way past my imagining. And repentance then becomes the regular recognition of how little we still understand what that truth means and how little we act upon it; of how unconverted we remain.

Go back to the Gospels and you will realise that what first caused people to repent and follow Jesus wasn't a recognition of their sinfulness, but the realisation for the first time in their lives that here is someone who sees into their hearts and loves and accepts them for what they are.

For example: there is the woman described in the Gospel as 'a notorious sinner' who comes into Simon's house while Jesus is having supper and anoints his feet with costly ointment and wipes them with her hair. She does so because she senses that he loves her as she is, and at once it draws out of her an answering love. And that enables Jesus then to say: 'Your sins are forgiven: go in peace'.

But note the order. 'We love because he first loved us' writes St John. So penitence doesn't spring from being made to feel guilty. Penitence is our amazed response to the true nature of God as that is made known in the life and the teaching, but even more in the suffering and death, of Jesus Christ.

I want you to be quite clear about what I am saying, because so many people have such strange and rather frightening ideas about God. What I am saying is what the New Testament proclaims: that when we say the words Jesus Christ we are claiming a totally new understanding of God. We no longer think of a God who surveys from some unimaginable distance in a dispassionate way, a world full of violence and pain where the innocent suffer and the weak go to the wall. For in Christ God himself is seen as one who shares the dirt and the pain and the bewilderment, the loneliness and the weakness, and even the darkness of a painful death. 'The crucified Jesus,' it has been said, 'is the only accurate picture of God the world has ever seen'.

In the trenches of the First World War, G.A. Studdert-Kennedy, who was a Chaplain and a poet, came across the mutilated body of a soldier in a shell-hole, a man to whom he had given Communion the previous day. Afterwards in a poem he wrote:

Father, if he the Christ were thy revealer
truly the first-begotten of the Lord,
then must *thou* be a sufferer and a healer,
pierced to the heart by the sorrow of the sword.

Each year, as we keep the forty days of Lent, and as we draw near to Passiontide, Holy Week and Good Friday, we are reminded not just of certain events in the long-distant past, but of what is happening daily. As those words were read in this morning's second lesson which told of Peter's denial and Christ's trial and imprisonment, some innocent man or woman was being battered, tortured or killed in some police station or barrack room somewhere in the world for no other reason than that he or she was at their mercy. The Passion of Jesus, the suffering of God, goes on, and we cannot plead that we are ignorant, or that it doesn't concern us, or that we are without blame.

On the eve of that first Good Friday Jesus was betrayed, not just by Judas, but also by Peter, whom he had chosen to be the leader of his church, Peter who stood by the fire and did nothing. And not only did nothing but, fearing for his own safety, denied he even knew him. And Jesus turned and looked at Peter ... and Peter went out and wept bitterly. I have no doubt it was because he saw in that look the love which had drawn him to Jesus from the beginning. The love which will not let us go despite our many acts of betrayal. And it is as we become aware of the sterling nature of that love that we become aware too of our sinfulness and find that forgiveness which is a kind of resurrection.

11

Remembering What We Truly Are

LENT 1992

St Margaret's Church, Westminster

The word Lent has a bleak sound to it. It suggests we're in for a lean time. It always seems to coincide with the Budget, and this year it's a Budget caught between the reality of the recession and the hype of an election. And all the parties seem to argue about is the economy, while each party is tempted to promise that in their hands stones will indeed miraculously become bread.

But 'man cannot live by bread alone', and man cannot live by economics alone, and there is no equation between money and contentment. Most people know this: few actually believe or live by it.

Jesus, of course, doesn't underrate the need for bread – for jobs and security and a roof over your head and a pension at the end of the day – he merely insists that it isn't enough. And it is the 'something more' that alone can meet the real need, the real ache in the human heart. And Lent is about stopping and examining afresh the nature of this 'something more'. It's about repenting, about a change of heart, about revising your values and redefining your goal. It's a time to ask some honest questions about who we are and what we're at.

Three years ago the Empress Zita of Austria/Hungary died aged ninety-seven. Her funeral was held in St Stephen's Cathedral, Vienna. When the cortège arrived the doors of the church were closed. The Chamberlain knocked three times with his staff and one of the friars inside called out 'Who requests entry?'

The reply was 'Her Majesty, Zita, Empress of Austria, Crowned Queen of Hungary, Queen of Bohemia, Dalmatia, Croatia, Slavonia, and Illyria, Archduchess of Austria, Grand Duchess of Tuscany ...' and so it went on ending with all her orders.

The friar replied: 'We do not know her. Who requests entry?' 'Her Majesty Zita Empress of Austria, Queen of Hungary.' Again the reply came: 'We do not know her. Who requests entry?' This time the Chamberlain replied: 'Our sister Zita, a poor, mortal sinner.' 'Let her enter!' And the doors were thrown open.

When Jesus commended the publican in the Temple whose only prayer was 'God have mercy on me a sinner', and when he called on people to repent, he wasn't asking them to grovel or feel guilty. He was asking them to be honest with themselves about their lives, to recognize the harm we do to ourselves and to others by our self-centredness, and to respond afresh to the love God has for each of us in our uniqueness as that love is seen in Christ. We are to repent not because we are afraid, and not because we are threatened, but because we are loved.

And, perhaps, above all, Jesus was asking them to open their eyes to their true destiny and to accept who they are: sons and daughters of God.

For Jesus, those temptations in the desert arise from his baptism. At that moment he understands who he is: he is aware of God saying to him, 'Thou art my Son'. But now he hears another voice: it says,

> 'If you are the Son of God, then how will you fulfil
> your vocation as God's Messiah? How will you make
> people listen? How will you use your powers? Surely,
> as the Son of God, you could win the gratitude of
> huge numbers of people by turning stones into bread;
> or you could win worldly power by leading the Zealots
> in armed insurrection against the Romans and become

a national hero; or you could test God by leaping
from the pinnacle of the Temple to the valley far
below knowing God will keep you safe, and so by
performing a spectacular trick compel people to
believe in you.'

And these are real temptations that come to Jesus as he
wrestles in the desert with the form his ministry is to take –
and he emerges knowing that if he is to reveal the true nature
of God he must show there is more to life than satisfying our
physical needs; that God's way is not the world's way; that
the way of self-giving love is always costly; and that God is to
be trusted, come what may, but not put to the test.

But I want to pursue what is to me a more intriguing
temptation. For note the words St Luke puts in the devil's
mouth: it's not *'because* you are the Son of God you could
choose to do this or that'. It's *'if'*. *'If* you are the Son of God';
it's a nagging, questioning doubt. 'Who am I?' That I believe
was the real desert experience for him. Was he really the
Messiah? Could he trust his deep inner conviction that
through him the Father was going to be revealed in a new and
unique way?

Now here is mystery we can only ponder, yet I find it a very
fruitful line of thought. Of course I am tempted – we all are –
to seek to live by bread alone. Of course I am tempted – we all
are – to live by worldly standards rather than God's. Of course
I am tempted – we all are – to put God to the test, to look for
special protection especially when sickness or danger
threaten. And it's all because *I doubt that I am really a child of
God.* That's the real temptation. My reluctance to become
what I truly am. My failure to grasp, to accept and to live by
the life-changing truth that I am a child of God, in St Paul's
words, 'an heir of God and a joint heir with Christ'. We are
sons and daughters of God, *'if* you are the Son of God'. Jesus
learned from his desert experience to accept both that he was

37

the 'Son of God' in a unique sense, and also what that meant in terms of faith and action: that is to say, in terms of trust and love.

'*If* you are sons and daughters of God'. It is in what we might think of as the desert experiences of life – in the dark times or the arid times – that we are tempted to doubt or despair; tempted to forget that the Christlike God is with us, that it is in him I live and move and have my being, that I am his child, come what may. And it is precisely in those times: in times of illness or bereavement, in times of loneliness or depression, in times when our prayer seems dead, that we need to affirm: 'I am in Christ: he is in me'. 'I am the child of God, made in his likeness.'

It isn't that we look to God to give us special protection in this unpredictable world. We Christians are not exempt from the lightning flash or the cancer cell, from accident or sudden death. If we leap off pinnacles of temples we shall be killed. God is not to be tested in that way. What it does mean is that we become those who say with Job, 'though he slay me, yet will I trust him'; or with the dying Jesus, 'Father, into your hands I commit my spirit.'

To be open to God is to achieve that kind of trust.

On Ash Wednesday some of us had ash placed on our forehead with the words: 'Remember that you are dust and to dust you shall return. Turn away from sin and be faithful to Christ'. Lent is not a bleak, forbidding time, but a very positive and optimistic remembering of what we truly are. 'Dust', but dust that dreams of glory; dust that has been claimed by God; dust that has a deep, aching sense both of its mortality and of its reaching after the God glimpsed in Jesus whom one day we shall see face to face.

12

The Healing Ministry and Counselling

LENT 1999

St Mary the Less Church, Cambridge

Nearly fifty years ago I arrived in Cambridge for the first time: in theory to read English at Corpus, in practice to spend my time acting. And sometimes, on a Sunday morning, I would come here for Mass. Twenty-five years later I came back for a second bite of the cherry: this time to be Vicar of your sister church, Great St Mary's, and to delight in the friendship of that inimitable and much-loved priest, Father James Owen. So Cambridge is an integral part of my journey.

But this strange thing we call memory plays tricks with time, so that as you grow old you remain the person you have always been, and this morning part of me is still the unconfident student sitting down there, near the back, wondering if I really approved of all those bells and smells; and part of me is the still unconfident but middle-aged Vicar of Great St Mary's delighting in one of James' May Week parties in the garden of 4 Newnham Terrace. It is this mystery that we call 'memory' that helps provide the unity and integrity that we need in our lives. Yet for many the memories are bad and destructive, their lives painful and fragmented. Which is why the shelves of Waterstone's and Dillons are crammed with books offering self-help and do-it-yourself spiritualities, and why one of the major growth areas of our fast-disappearing century has been that of counselling.

The chief purpose of most secular, non-directive counselling is to enable you to understand why you are what you are, to come to terms with your past so that you may live with confidence in the present and find the right path into the future. It is therefore a combination of therapy, comfort, affirmation and guidance. My task this morning is to ask what we mean by counselling as it relates to the Church's healing ministry. And while such counselling will aim to be therapeutic, comforting and affirming, its ultimate purpose is to help people understand where they are and to be given some vision of that wholeness that is God's purpose for each of us.

All counselling demands certain qualities in the counsellor. The first is the ability to listen. The art of listening is a rare and therapeutic one: giving attention to another person, because you know that persons are not problems to be solved but mysteries to be loved, is harder than it sounds. It demands two of our most impressive qualities: *empathy*, the craft of trying to get inside someone else's world, feeling what it is like to be him or her at that moment. And *compassion*, that word which literally means 'suffering alongside', the readiness to give both time and attention to a person, which may enable them to feel – perhaps for the first time in their lives – that what they do and say and feel *matters*. What good counsellors say, by their attention and their silence is: 'You matter. You are of unique value. What you have to tell me about your own human story is so important that I don't want to miss a single fact or nuance of it.' How better can we convey the worth and affirm the true value of another human being?

And there we touch on the very heart of the matter: this readiness to share our own humanity, our own vulnerability, our own journey. For while each of us is wonderfully unique, yet the story of your human journey is in its most resonant depths my story as well, for there is a larger story that unites us all. Humanity, it has been said, is like an enormous spider's web: if you touch it anywhere, you set the whole thing trembling.

There is a poem by the Welsh poet-priest R.S. Thomas called 'The Word'. It is, as you would expect, bleak.

> A pen appeared, and the god said:
> 'Write what it is to be
> man.' And my hand hovered
> long over the bare page,
> until there, like footprints
> of the lost traveller, letters
> took shape on the page's
> blankness, and I spelled out
> the word 'lonely'. And my hand moved
> to erase it; but the voices
> of all those waiting at life's
> window cried out loud: 'It is true.'

The story we share, this larger story that unites us all, alternates between the twin poles of loneliness and community. It speaks of the unpredictability of human life, of the brokenness, failure, anger, guilt and pain, that are implicit in the costly business of loving and being loved. Anyone who has counselled another knows that listening – proper listening – to another in their confusion or pain or search for meaning awakens all kinds of echoes in yourself, and that this recognition is the beginning of compassion. The loneliness has been met. A gulf has been bridged between one human being and another. It may be, of course, that the most an effective counsellor can do is agree with someone eaten up by loneliness that loneliness is indeed part of what it means to be human. But to *be there* – and to go on being there – for them, may enable them to find healing in facing their loneliness at a level where it can be shared. For in the end to be human is not to be lonely, but to be part of a process which we call *community*.

Yet for Christians counselling is not just about countering human loneliness, for we have a more profound story to tell,

41

one which resonates in all our personal stories and pulls them together and makes sense of them. It's a story that acknowledges the voice that lies deep within the human heart and cries out for meaning and value, for some vision that meets our bewildered questions and gives us a framework within which we may live with integrity. I guess we can bear almost any suffering provided – and only provided – we can discern some meaning in it that may redeem it. I do not know who counselled Nelson Mandela, but his readiness to forgive and his creative use of what might have been bitter, wasted years is strikingly true to the teaching of Jesus about the healing power of forgiveness and the meaning of resurrection and new life.

Now there is such a story, one that embraces all our stories. It hangs upon two other poles, those of creation and redemption. It tells of the God who creates a universe with an end and a purpose. But a universe, in St Paul's words, that is at present frustrated and

> 'groans as if in the pangs of childbirth ... (but one)
> that is to be freed from the shackles of mortality
> and enter upon the glorious liberty of the children of
> God.'

So it tells, this greater story, of God's way of re-creating us and winning us back to himself. Its plot hangs on three events: Christmas, Good Friday and Easter. It's not a story of a God who answers all our puzzled questions about the mystery of things, but of one who instead himself enters into those questions and in so doing transforms them. We are invited to identify our pain, our vulnerability, our suffering with that of the Christlike God who enters fully into the human condition and becomes one with us. For if it is true, as this morning's Gospel says, that 'God so loved the world that he gave his only Son' then we must be willing to have our understanding of God profoundly changed. Here is a God who shares the dirt and the pain; and knows from the inside our weakness, loneliness and death. And the presence of Jesus once in history was the presence of God as he has always been and will always be. Christlike.

For forty years I have sought, as every priest does, to counsel those hurt by life. I've sat with the dying, tried to console the bereaved, spent hour upon hour encouraging the unloved and listening to the wounded and the lonely. And all I know is that, time and again, the only words that have helped have had to do with the concept of the suffering God, whose love for us cannot be altered or diminished; with Christ crucified, the Christ who, even in his risen life, still bears in his hands the marks of the nails and the wound in his side.

In the end the pastoral and counselling ministry of the Church is there to help all of us find comfort, healing and forgiveness. To enable us to see our human story in the light of that other story which touches on ours at every point. For it speaks of how our lives may be changed, re-woven into a new pattern. In the end, of course, it is not we who do this. It is God who does it by affirming, in the person of Jesus Christ, that we may walk through this uncertain and chancy world as those who are loved. For if you know you are loved your past is forgiven, your present affirmed, and your future full of hope.

13

The Costly Way of Love

PASSION SUNDAY 1989

Westminster Abbey

And Jesus replied: 'Unless a grain of wheat falls into the earth and dies, it remains alone; but if it dies, it bears much fruit.'

When Jesus makes the final decision of his life, and sets out on his last journey to Jerusalem, he is deliberately choosing the costly way of suffering. He is triggering events that will take their inexorable course until this most kingly of men is betrayed, arrested, tortured, tried and executed like a common criminal: his throne a cross, his crown a crown of thorns.

So it is that on this Passion Sunday, we enter upon the two most solemn weeks of the Christian year; and begin once again to explore something more of how the mystery of human suffering is illuminated by the death on the cross of this man we claim as our king.

When you and I were baptized something at first sight very surprising happened to us. The priest placed on our forehead the sign of that cross. And what that says in the clearest possible way is that those who choose to follow the way of Christ will not be spared the pain and suffering that come to all human beings. It suggests that we can learn much from the way Jesus met his own suffering and death and retained his trust in God even in the worst kind of desolation.

But this cross with which we are each marked is also a statement of a more subtle and challenging kind. For it says that the sign that I have come of age as a Christian will be when I begin to understand what Jesus meant when he said that anyone who clings to his life will lose it and anyone who dies to himself will live; that you cannot truly live unless you are first prepared to die.

Jesus never ceased to offer people the consolation of knowing that each was loved and valued by God, but neither did he pretend that to be his disciple isn't costly in one way or another. He consoled, but he also challenged.

For he invites us to do battle on two fronts.

First, he asks me to come to terms with my own ego, my own self-centredness, so that I may die to its clamourous demands and in time, and by God's grace, come to express in my own words and actions Christ's own way of self-giving love.

St Paul takes up this theme when, in today's Epistle, he urges all who have been baptized to learn to 'die daily' so that 'you may be raised to life with Christ through your faith in the active power of God'.

But there is a second way in which we as followers of Christ are marked with the cross. Jesus didn't suffer and die from a terminal illness. He was killed because what he knew to be the truth about God and man and what is of ultimate value caused him to speak and act in a way which caused the leaders in church and state to respond with violence. He suffered because he refused to compromise with evil or conform to the standards and values of the world. And in the end he died because there was no other way to prove how far love and truth are prepared to go.

That is why the cross, and the figure of Christ dying on the cross, is not simply the most haunting image of human sinfulness and God's loving response, but also the most powerful instrument for change in the world. Were there time I could speak of the very many men and women, known and unknown, whose lives of non-violent and courageous resistance to injustice and oppression have witnessed to the Passion of Christ in our own time – not least in Africa. Yet the costly way of Jesus is not confined to the heroes of the faith: it follows from our Baptism, and for us it may mean the readiness to choose *that* job rather than *this* one; the readiness to forgive a wrong; the readiness to name those values – however unpopular – on which we will stand firm, and for which we are ready to suffer and, if need be, to die.

Today, as we begin another Passiontide and Holy Week, I would ask you as you leave the Abbey to look carefully at the striking sculpture in the Nave, a sculpture of the hand of Christ pierced by a nail; and then reflect on what we have done at this service. At the Last Supper Jesus took the bread in his hands and broke it before he shared it. And when we do the same each week at the Eucharist, we are saying, *by this act of breaking*, that the way of Jesus is the way of being broken, the way of sacrifice, of letting the protective shell of our lives be broken so that we may live for others. For Jesus that meant the Cross. And we too, in receiving the broken bread, are committing ourselves to a life which, if it is to conform in any way to his, is bound to reflect the costly way of love.

14

The Hands of Jesus

TUESDAY OF HOLY WEEK 1994

Westminster Abbey

At the end of the nave there stands this week a modern sculpture of the hand of Christ. It is striking – some find it disturbing – because of the nail driven through the palm. It is the hand of the crucified Christ raised in blessing, and so it is the hand of the risen Christ, speaking of both Good Friday and Easter.

Very briefly I want to point you, on this Tuesday of Holy Week, to the hands of Jesus.

The hands of Jesus were a workman's hands which knew the feel of wood in the carpenter's shop. He had used his hands to heal the sick, to bless and to absolve the sinful. He had used his hands, at the Last Supper, to wash and dry his disciples' dusty feet. Into his hands he had taken the bread that he likened to his body, and had given thanks over it, broken it and handed it to his friends.

And then, on that Friday, they had taken his hands and nailed them to a Cross shaped by another carpenter.

After God had raised him from the dead, Jesus had shown his scarred hands to Thomas when he doubted the resurrection, and invited him to touch his wounds.

Six hundred years before the birth of Jesus Isaiah put into the mouth of God these remarkable words as God speaks of how much he values us: 'You are mine and I love you. Look, I have engraved you on the palm of my hands.'

As you pass that hand of Christ when you leave the Abbey, having been fed at this Eucharist, having received the living bread into the palm of your hands, see that sculpted hand as that of the risen Christ holding his hand over you in blessing; but then go on to see the nail scarring that hand as a sign of the limits to which a Christ-like God is prepared to go in order to bring us to our senses, and to bring home to us the nature of his love. And be thankful.

15

The God Who is All Love

MAUNDY THURSDAY 1997

Salisbury Cathedral

Jesus smiled.

'You call me Lord,' he said. 'So I am. That is why I
wash your feet,
So should you too serve one another.
The master is not greater than his servant.
But the servant is not greater than his master ...
Only by serving others can we help ourselves,
Only by kneeling do we grow taller –'
as usual his paradox bewildered them, and produced
an embarrassed silence.

The words of the playwright, Ronald Duncan. Paradox
indeed, and which of us is not bewildered by it?

There is the paradox of this service, placed at the critical
point of Holy Week, in which we journey from a joyful
eucharistic celebration into the darkness of the betrayal and
arrest in Gethsemane.

There is the paradox of the one of whom John the Baptist
said that he (John) was not worthy to kneel and unfasten the
strap of his sandals now stooping to wash his disciples' feet.
There is the paradox of the unimaginable majesty of God
matched only by the force of his awesome love. And the
paradox of the traditional concept of power and authority
being turned on its head and redefined as the humble service
of one another.

We need to come to the events of this extraordinary week with the clear eyes of an artist or a child. For while they speak of profound mysteries that fill the world's libraries with theological speculation, they also contain utterly simple truths of the sort that speak to the heart; the kind of truth which may be very familiar, heard a thousand times, and yet a truth that does not become ours, until it is felt on our pulses and is part of our life-blood, until we can say: 'Now I see, now I understand; and the knowledge has changed me.'

I suppose if you had asked St John why his gospel is so different from the others, why (for example) he omits the description of the Last Supper and replaces it with the story of Jesus washing his disciples' feet, he might have said: 'Because my purpose is quite simple. It is to offer a profound reflection upon what it means to be loved by God.' What it means to have seen his glory in the Word made flesh, a glory 'full of grace and truth'. Yet a glory that is not too dazzling for human eyes to contemplate, for it is a glory that is revealed when Jesus kneels at John's feet and begins to wash them. There could be no more menial action, no more shocking definition of what loving each other entails, no more dramatic encapsulation of the new understanding of God, than in their Lord and master kneeling at their feet on the night of his arrest.

In what is perhaps the most perceptive religious poem in the language, George Herbert's *Love bade me welcome*, Herbert at first protests that he is unworthy of a place at the Lord's table:

> 'I, the unkind, ungrateful? Ah, my dear,
> I cannot look on Thee.'
> Love took my hand and smiling did reply,
> 'Who made the eyes but I?'

> 'Truth, Lord, but I have marr'd them: let my shame
> Go where it doth deserve.'
> 'And know you not', says Love, 'Who bore the blame?'

So gradually he is persuaded that he is accepted, forgiven and loved, and he responds as Peter responds, though with more courtesy:

'My dear, then I will *serve*.'

And he has missed the point. George Herbert is not called upon to serve but to *be served*. Peter is not called upon to wash the feet of others – not at that stage – but to let his Lord wash his feet. And he vigorously protests: '*You*, washing *my* feet? Never!' Those are the words of a man who suddenly finds all the familiar assumptions of his life overturned, yet who in the next moment knows he must give in – or go away. Peter yielded and stayed: it was Judas who left.

We have just witnessed the foot-washing being symbolically acted out, first by the Dean as leader of our community, and then by others in their turn. But to interpret this action simply as an injunction to love one another in acts of caring service may be to miss the whole point. For, complex creatures that we are, our motives are often questionable and such service can often be a subtly-disguised form of pride. And the origin of our Christian journey, and its motivation, has to be our readiness not to give, but to receive. 'We love' writes St John, (that is to say, 'We are capable to love') 'because he first loved us.' It is immediately after he has washed their feet that Jesus says to those gathered round the table: 'Love one another as I have loved you,' and indeed, as he has shown them to be loved by his Father. And another way of saying that is: 'Go about your life as those who are loved.'

I guess we believe it, this deepest truth of all; this knowledge that if we are each accepted, forgiven, loved and valued by our Creator then it opens our eyes to one another's worth, and sets us free to reach out to each other in service and friendship and love.

And yet we are only half-persuaded, and need, over and over again, to repent of our lack of faith and little love, and let another Holy Week speak to us afresh of the God who is all love and will do everything to win us to himself.

Does My Creator Weep?

GOOD FRIDAY 1996

Westminster Abbey

Words from St Matthew's account of the crucifixion: 'And they sat down and watched him there.'

I know a man whose eleven-year-old son died in the middle of the night from a sudden attack of asthma. It was a shocking, totally unexpected death. His father chose to keep a record of his grief, written in the form of letters to be read one day by his older child. He describes the first weeks of numbness and disbelief, the aching sense of loss, his overwhelming anger that life could end so abruptly for one who had everything to live for. It makes him rage against God that other children thrive and play. A sudden glimpse of a boy in town with a bird-like frame and blond hair 'rocks my blood'.

And then, after a bit, he wants to know *why*? 'I have sat alone in many churches' he writes, 'and felt the quiet enter into me. The quiet of minds that believed, and still believe. The coloured windows, the candles; the man hanging on a Cross.' And he asks: 'Does my creator weep?'

It is a Job-like question: a question for the raped women and orphaned children of Bosnia, a question for the man being tortured at this instant in some police cell in some terrorist regime; a question for the limbless children in Cambodia, or, coming nearer home, for the parents of those innocent victims of the horrifying slaughter in Dunblane. 'Does my creator weep?' It is above all a Good Friday question. For it can only be answered by the man hanging on the Cross who desires to show us the aching heart of God.

So let us consider the crucified on this day when the Passion of Jesus reveals the compassion of the Father.

Jesus, whose life-giving words were listened to by some with wonder and delight and by others with anger and incomprehension, spoke as much about suffering as about joy. He had said that it is only in our giving of ourselves, in our letting go and dying to ourselves, that true happiness is to be found. He had spoken of the need to respond to hatred and persecution with forgiveness and love, and to trust the Father whatever may come. Now they are killing him, slowly and painfully. How will he respond?

So they watch him. As they have watched him turn to face Jerusalem, watched him cleanse the temple of the money-changers, watched his agony in the garden, watched him stand trial and undergo torture. And now they watch him most especially on the Cross: a handful who love him, but many more who are indifferent or dismissive: 'They sat down and watched him there.'

And what do they see? They see his compassion. As the nails are driven home and soldiers string him up and the crowds mock him, he responds with the words: 'Father, forgive them, they know not what they do.' And then, a little later, they see his apparent dereliction. They hear the words: 'My God, my God, why hast thou forsaken me?' For, as the darkness deepens, Jesus feels the intimate presence of God with which he has always lived is being withdrawn. And in that cry can be heard every human cry of anguish and loneliness and despair, then and now. Here is a man like us raging against the dying of the light, a deep human protest against such terrible and pointless waste as a premature death from cancer, or ethnic cleansing, or an act of destructive violence. Does my Creator weep? Does he even exist?

Now it is not for a preacher on Good Friday to come up with slick and easy answers to such questions. Indeed, those

54

who first speak of the death of Jesus in the light of Easter know they are handling events which are ultimately a profound mystery. Yet what the gospel claims is that if you press more and more deeply into the darkness you discover at the heart of it the man hanging on the Cross, the man who is human in the fullest sense, and yet for those who have the eye of faith something more. For what the gospel claims is that if we wish to know what God is like, how he is present in his world, then this is the place to look. For this man was so open to the Father's love, so uniquely close to the Father's heart, that in St John's words, 'He has made him known.'

One of the hymns we sang earlier includes these words:

> Therefore he who shows us God
> helpless hangs upon the tree;
> and the nails and crown of thorns
> tell of what God's love must be.
>
> Here is God: no monarch he
> throned in easy state to reign;
> here is God, whose arms of love
> aching, spent, the world sustain.

Over the centuries there have been some strange and unappealing theories about the sacrificial death of Christ. They have seemed to suggest that the Passion and death of Jesus are some kind of pagan sacrifice: that he comes to placate an angry God, or to submit to an inscrutable and cruel God who requires his blood. On the contrary: in Jesus God is revealed – and there is no more profound mystery or more wonderful truth – as one who speaks our language and shares our life. God doesn't answer our bewildered questions, but somehow, in the Word made flesh, he enters into the heart of those questions himself. What Jesus came to do, and nowhere more powerfully than in his death, is to embody the love of God for his creation. In the words of John Austin Baker: 'The crucified

Jesus is the only accurate picture of God the world has ever seen, and the hands that hold us in existence are pierced with unimaginable nails.'

This is how the bridge is restored between God and us. We are at one with God again, and so we speak of the Atonement – literally, the *at-one-ment*, the reconciliation: 'God was in Christ reconciling the world to himself.' Not by *changing* his attitude to his creatures, but by revealing it unmistakably as it truly is. Jesus is for ever the outward and visible sign of what God's love is like.

'And they sat down and watched him there.' When you consider the first disciples were witnessing a bloody cruci-fixion, isn't it remarkable that when they looked back at the dreadful things that had happened to their Lord it brought them to a new awareness, not simply (as you would expect) of the love of Jesus, but of the love of God.

Now, despite Good Friday, I don't believe we shall ever fully know in this life the answer to the question *why* there is undeserved suffering and evil. But since Good Friday we do know the answer to an equally profound question: How can it be used and redeemed? For with God on our side, and in the spirit of Jesus, we can take the chaotic, meaningless raw material of suffering and fashion it and make use of it. When suffering comes you enter a kind of dark valley of self-pity and despair; yet beyond them there is another country where what is evil may begin to be redeemed. And those words of desolation from Psalm 22, 'My God, my God, why have you forsaken me?' are the starting-point of a psalm that goes on to a reassertion of faith and the conviction that ultimately the whole world will acknowledge that God is good and to be trusted. And so, as Jesus' sense of the goodness of God comes into focus again, he is at last able to give the great shout of triumph: 'It is accomplished' and to die with his own inti-mate, affectionate word for God – 'Abba, Father' – on his lips: 'Father, into thy hands I commend my spirit'. And so the man who has taught them that not a sparrow falls to the ground without the Father's knowledge, shows that for him death itself is included in the divine Fatherliness; that like every other experience in life it is an opportunity, the final opportunity, to show that God is to be trusted, that 'all shall be well, and all manner of things shall be well.'

As I grow older I believe more and more that this world is a place above all for learning how to love and how to trust. To sit and watch Jesus on his Cross, to hear his words and observe the manner of his dying, is to see what that loving, trusting relationship with the Father really means. Yet the Cross is not just to be looked at. It is to be seized, entered into and made our own. It is stamped on our forehead at baptism: it is the way to which we are committed. And to be a Christian means to belong to the community which tries to live like Jesus: with his costly kind of loving, his costly kind of giving, his costly kind of thankfulness and his costly kind of trust. If we can begin to learn to live like this, if we can meet suffering like this, if in the end we can face our own death like this, then the Spirit of Jesus lives in us and we in him in all the power of his crucified and risen life.

In the end Good Friday is not a day for words. It's a day for silence and penitence; a day when we can drop our pretences as we stand or kneel at the foot of the Cross, admitting the weakness of our faith, our lack of trust and our little love; asking for God's forgiveness, acknowledging his goodness and responding to his grace.

17

My Lord and My God

EASTER DAY 1993

Westminster Abbey

Some words of William Blake: 'Unless the eye catch fire, the God will not be seen.'

When St John attempts to describe the indescribable, the morning of Christ's Resurrection, he wants us to see the central truth that has changed his life. So he chooses the word 'see' and he picks two Greek verbs for the word 'see' that have different meanings.

He tells of how Peter and John run to the tomb. John outruns Peter, gets there first and, peeping in, *sees* the grave clothes, but dares not go further. Peter goes in and he too *sees* the grave clothes. There the Gospel writer is using 'see' in the first sense, as I might say 'I see you sitting before me'.

But then John looks more closely, and suddenly the penny drops and he understands for the first time the significance of what he is seeing, and, writes St John, 'he *saw* and believed.'

That is to see in the second sense: to perceive, to know a truth deep within you, as I might say 'I *see* why you are here on Easter Day: I understand that we are together drawn to this place by our shared belief in the risen Christ.'

For what John saw and understood wasn't that the body of Jesus had disappeared. What he saw was that this Jesus was indeed the Christ, the Son of God, and that death could not hold him in its power.

In the 13th century those who built this Abbey placed before our eyes on that wall in Poets' Corner the scene of St

Thomas with the risen Jesus in the Upper Room. Thomas had not been present on that first Easter night and had said that he would not believe unless he saw the risen Jesus with his own eyes. A week later he was there when Jesus appeared and he saw and believed. What matters is not that Thomas sees the wounds in Jesus' hands and side but that he sees and understands. And so his response is not 'What a remarkable event – a dead body come back to life' but quite simply 'My Lord and my God'. His eyes had been opened to what God has done: they are living, as it were, in the first days of a new creation.

'Unless the eye catch fire, the God will not be seen' wrote Blake; and he went on 'unless the heart catch fire, the God will not be loved.'

If, looking at Jesus Christ, we can say 'My Lord and my God' then we are indeed the Easter people, those who believe that, in Jesus' words, 'You who have seen me have seen the Father'; those who see in the Cross and the empty tomb all we need to know of the Father's power and the Father's love.

In wishing you a joyful Easter I pray that you may see and understand afresh the power of God to create and to redeem; and that we may each know, within and among us, the Spirit of the risen Christ.

18

Christ is In Our Midst

EASTER DAY 1994

Westminster Abbey

God save us from the extremists, be they Islamic mullahs out for the blood of Salman Rushdie, tub-thumping Irish politicians, violent nationalists, or even certain born-again Christians on the rampage who have you diving for cover.

But God save us, equally, from the bland, the unsurprising, the undemanding and the inoffensive. I think of Yeats' lines:

> The best lack all conviction, while the worst
> Are full of passionate intensity.

To stand in this pulpit on Easter Day, with a message at once familiar in its content and breath-taking in its claim, is to be faced by this quandary. To repeat the familiar words about the empty tomb and tell the familiar stories can seem, in a scientific and worldly-wise age, to be mere pulpit-talk and lack all conviction; nor will any amount of passionate intensity make the mystery more credible. We have, it seems to me, to start elsewhere.

One fact determines whether or not you are a religious person, and it has little to do with your education, your creed or your culture. At its simplest, it is this: do you see your life as a miracle? Do you see the marvel that is every leaf of every tree and every blade of grass? Do you see the marvel of every cell in your body, each carrying the genes that determine your precise uniqueness? Do you see the marvel of every thought in that mysterious electrochemical system that is your brain; or reflect on the dance of atoms in their electric field in what we call matter? Do you take all this mystery and miracle for granted, or do you look on it with a kind of amazed wonder? Isaac Newton once said: 'In the absence of any other proof the thumb alone will convince me of God's existence'; and Albert Einstein wrote: 'Whoever is devoid of the capacity to wonder might just as well be dead.'

I think it was Donald Soper who was once proclaiming the Gospel at Speakers' Corner in Hyde Park and talking one day of the wonder of God's creation. 'What about the wonder of science?' said a heckler, 'Give me the right equipment and I could do some of that.' 'OK' said Soper quietly, 'make us a rabbit, just to give us confidence'.

Do you take rabbits for granted – or babies, or Mozart, or that amazing roof? Do you take love for granted? Or courage, or compassion? Or do you see, in all the mystery that is you, and in the creation, sufficient glimpses of the unimaginable power of the creator to cause you to think out afresh what is and might be possible?

The great turning points in human thought – and the first Easter is one of them – are when a group of individuals are made to wonder and go on wondering, because of some event or experience they can't deny; an experience in this case that changes their understanding of what is possible, and reshapes their ideas of God.

Long before the Gospel writers told the Easter stories (of the empty tomb and the appearances of the risen Christ) St Paul wrote his Letters. They don't include those stories – no empty tomb, no upper room – and if you had asked him why I think he would have said: 'I'm not concerned with the mystery of *when*? or *where*? or *how*? I am concerned with the reality of the experience and the *now*.' 'All I know', he would say, 'is Christ and the power of his risen life, and it is an experience that has caused me to rethink what I believe to be possible and entirely change my idea of God.'

What he had been blind to and now saw with an astonished and grateful wonder is that there is no limit to God's power to create and to redeem, to recreate and to affirm his creatures. It is, after all, the essence of love to affirm the beloved. Not even death can abort God's purpose for us. For God is not a monster. He's a lover. He doesn't offer us the miraculous gift of life only to snatch it back again. He doesn't create us in his image only to have that image smashed beyond repair. He doesn't reveal himself in Jesus to prove what we already know – that life is unjust and death cruel and sometimes violent. He comes to affirm that what he creates will not in the end be destroyed.

There is a reading popular at memorial services by Henry Scott Holland which begins: 'Death is nothing at all'. That is clearly nonsense. Death is momentous, a going into the dark, the end of all we know. But what Easter proclaims is a God who has made of me a creature of flesh *and* spirit, unique and therefore precious to him, and who will not let me go. To be a Christian is to trust that God is able to recreate, to raise up, this being I call 'me' in some new, unimaginable way; that in Christ I am called into a relationship with God that not only goes to the very depths of my being, but also extends beyond my death.

If this morning I neglect the traditional Easter stories of the Gospels for the earlier witness of St Paul's 'All I know is Christ and the power of his risen life', it is because like him I want to point you away from the *when* and *where* and *how*, to the reality of the experience in the moment that is *now*. No other event, no other experience, has so changed the face of history. The experience of Resurrection, the knowledge that Jesus Christ was in their midst as a life-giving Spirit, created the Church. No Easter: no Abbey. Indeed, no Easter: no Christianity. It's as simple as that. In Christ crucified and risen God does something quite new. He makes us rethink who we are and what our ultimate end is to be. For, to quote St Paul again, 'If anyone is united to Christ there is a new creation.'

Today all over the world millions of Christians are celebrating the resurrection, not as a *past* event, something in the Bible, but as a *now* event: a relationship with the Christ-like God in whom we live and who lives in us, just as powerful now as he ever was to open our blind eyes and unstop our deaf ears and set us free from the prisons of our own making and, as it were, raise us from the dead and give us new life.

Once again we are at this point linking Easter with baptism, as the early and medieval Church always did. Baptism is the way in which, by turning to Christ, we pass from death to new life and attempt to live as part of the new creation – and there is no other day that speaks to us so powerfully of that truth.

The Orthodox Church, in its Easter words of greeting, goes to the heart of it: 'Christ is in our midst!' and the reply 'He is, and always will be!' *That* is the reality that I profess, with conviction if not with passionate intensity; and it is in that Easter faith that I hope to die, and so pass with Christ from death to life.

19

Our Human Journey

EASTER SEASON 1998

The Church of Sts Peter and Paul, Clare

It's a truism that you can only live your life forwards but you can only understand it backwards; and as you grow older you begin to see that there are certain people who have been absolutely central to your journey: a teacher, perhaps, who for you unlocked some magic world; or a priest, who was there at the right moment, and helped to affirm you when things seemed to be falling apart. But there are also people who, because they happen to have been in the right place at the right time, have acted as a kind of catalyst in your life. I am here because 35 years ago Barbara Potts – whose home is in Clare, and who has probably never featured in a sermon before and no doubt hopes she never will again – held a party and introduced me to my wife. That totally changed for both of us the nature of our journey. And your vicar, before he was so distressingly struck down by illness, heard that we would be staying with Barbara this weekend and thought he would seize the chance of grabbing a passing dean. So much by explanation.

It is about our human journey that I want to speak; or rather, about its destination, for that's where today's collect, epistle and gospel all point. St Paul writes of us desiring to 'have the new body' which God will provide put on over our present mortal body, 'so that our mortal part may be absorbed into life immortal'. For, he adds, 'God has shaped us for this very end'. And in the gospel Jesus says: 'Trust in God always; trust also in me. There are many dwelling-places in my Father's house ....'

When I was young and knew little of the world, a wise, if inquisitive, man asked me: 'What are you going to do with your life?' 'I want to be an actor' I said, 'or just possibly a priest.' 'Yes' he said, 'and what then?' 'Well, then I hope to get a fulfilling job and marry and have children.' 'And what then?' 'Then I suppose I'll retire and cultivate my garden, and preach in lovely towns like Clare.' 'And what then?' he persisted. 'Then, though I can't really imagine that far, I guess I'll die.' 'And what then?' I should have replied, though I was far too polite: 'I haven't the faintest idea – and neither have you!' But now I'm not so sure. For now, with my increasing years, I find I have all sorts of clues to an answer, and they all point in the same hopeful direction and to one hopeful destination. They all point to home.

I have a wonderful friend, an American novelist called Frederick Buechner. In a recent book called *The Longing for Home* he wrote this:

> I cannot claim that I have found the home I long for
> every day of my life, not by a long shot, but I believe
> that in my heart I have found, and have maybe
> always known, the way that leads to it. I believe that
> the home we long for and belong to is finally where
> Christ is. I believe that home is Christ's kingdom,
> which exists both within us and among us as we
> wend our prodigal ways through the world in search
> of it.

There is in the Orthodox funeral service a lovely phrase in which the priest prays that the departed may have found his or her 'desired homeland'; for, in Paul's words, 'our home-land is in heaven'. How then are we to speak of that home-land? My head gives one answer; my heart another. My head tells me that there is no way in which I can know anything that lies beyond the grave: that, again in the words of St Paul, 'no eye has seen, no ear has heard, and none can imagine what God has prepared for those who love him.' And my brain goes on to tell me that a land of endless sunshine may be a travel agent's delight, the perfect holiday haunt; but that endless sensual pleasure, incessant music for massed harps and heavenly choirs, would become as quickly boring as the surely tedious practice of 'casting down our golden crowns about the glassy sea'.

But my heart tells me something quite different. My heart tells me that there must be an end, a design, a purpose to our lives, and that somehow that meaning is linked to the most important lessons we have to learn here on earth: they are, quite simply, how to love and how to trust. My heart tells me that because I am human, created in the likeness of my Creator, there is in me a deep, unsatisfied hunger. It isn't a hunger for anything that money can buy. It's a kind of homesickness: a longing for wholeness, for the bringing to fruition, the fulfilment, of that potential for love, those stirrings of compassion, that response to beauty, those intimations of joy, that have prompted me all my life in my search for God, and drawn me inevitably, as iron filings are drawn to magnetic north, in the direction of home.

I know that there is in me, as I know that there is in you, a longing to become my true self, set free to love and be loved, to know and be known, to forgive and be forgiven; and that this longing is at root a hunger for God who is the source of all our glimpses of beauty, truth and goodness. St Augustine was right: 'our hearts *are* restless until they rest in Thee'. And one day that hunger will be satisfied. To hope for heaven or the City of God is simply to set our hunger in the context of eternity where, again in St Augustine's words, 'we shall rest and we shall see; we shall see and we shall love; we shall love and we shall praise; in the end which is no end.'

And those words, 'rest', 'see' and 'love', give us a further clue to what heaven will be like. We shall find *rest* at last from our fussy self-centredness, anxiety and self-concern. We shall *see* truths about our own value and each other's value in God's sight which will set us free to *love*; and heaven will see the fulfilment of all our human relationships which here on earth are often so messy and inadequate and incomplete. And what is so striking about the Christian (as opposed to say the Buddhist) concept of heaven is that we shall not lose our separate identities, merged like drops of water in some amorphous sea. Rather, we shall still be our unique, irreplaceable selves; and those words of the lover to the beloved, 'I love you because you are you', which were such a remarkable aspect of the ministry of Jesus, will describe God's relationship with each one of us for ever.

'Trust in God always; trust also in me.' Learning how to love; learning how to trust. How to trust that underlying all the unpredictability of life on earth, when an accident or a sudden illness can send us spinning, stronger than sin and evil and even the power of death itself, are those everlasting arms that sustain the world. And the clue to such a spirit of trust is, in those words of Frederick Buechner which I quoted just now,

> to believe in our hearts ... that the home we long for and belong to is finally where Christ is. I believe that home is Christ's kingdom, which exists both within us and among us as we wend our prodigal ways through the world in search of it.

For what God has done in Christ, what we call Easter and what the New Testament calls 'the new creation', is as dramatic and literally life-changing as the original creation of the world. What Jesus offers to those whose eyes are opened is a new and quite different quality of life, so that when they look at him they see the Fatherly love of God. And this new kind of life is called 'eternal', because it isn't measured in terms of linear time: those seconds and minutes and hours and days that for us finally come to a shuddering halt when we draw our last breath. It begins here and now and it is measured rather in the way we measure our deepest relationships: in terms of depth and quality; in terms of trust and confidence and love; except that this relationship with God, once entered into, is binding and goes even deeper, and his covenant with us is not for this life only but for ever.

It was said of Jesus by the Danish philosopher, Kierkegaard, that he was a man who lived his life and faced his death totally without anxiety because 'he had eternity with him in the day that is called today' and that therefore the future had no power over him. It is in *that* sense that we are to live as those who so know and trust the love that God has for us that we do already begin to taste here and now something of that quality of life which is what life with God will ultimately be.

And so it's futile to speculate about life after death or the unimaginable life of heaven: it's also unnecessary. For being a Christian isn't about earning our fulfilment in heaven or avoiding that ultimate loneliness that is hell. It's about responding to the Christ-like God revealed by Jesus, and so discovering the God in whose likeness we are made and whose life is within us all. And so entering into a relationship of love and trust of such a quality that nothing has the power to destroy it. What alone rings true, as we reflect on the meaning and mystery of our life and death, rings true to the promises of Jesus; rings true to everything we know about the nature of love; rings true to our own experience of loving and being loved; and rings true to our own deepest instincts that the essence of love is to affirm the right of the beloved to exist.

In Jesus God does just that. He affirms each one of us in all the mystery of our being. And what God affirms nothing can contradict or deny. That is the hope with which Christians faced the last Millennium and with which we face the new one. That is the hope that gives meaning to what often feels like an uncertain future in a meaningless world.

I began by speaking of those rare individuals who touch and change our lives. One who did that for me was a priest who died much too young of cancer. Each night during the final months of his life he and his wife said together today's collect. In it we ask God to

> give us grace,
> to love what you command
> and to desire what you promise,
> that in all the changes and chances of this world,
> our hearts may surely there be fixed
> where lasting joys are to be found ....

If we dare to call ourselves the Easter people, it is because we do most deeply desire God's promise: that our true homeland is in heaven. And, when you think of it, what more could God have done than to come where we are, and in the person of his Son take us by the hand in order to lead us home?

20

Easter People

EASTER SEASON 2004

Truro Cathedral

I have good memories of Cornwall. I grew to love it in my early teenage years. It was wartime, and my school was evacuated to the Carlyon Bay Hotel, and I have the clearest memory of coming to this cathedral in 1944 to sing treble in Haydn's *Creation*. Fifty years later, in 1994, I came back to preach in early summer for the Three Spires Festival service. Just before the service one of the canons said he was really extremely sorry but, having informed his computer a few days previously that wherever the word 'May' occurred with a capital M it was to replace it with the word 'June', I appeared on the service sheet, not as 'Michael Mayne' but as 'Michael June-ne'.

As you grow older you come to see that even the simplest things are more mysterious than you once thought, depending on how much attention you pay to them. For example, what could be more ordinary than dust? Yet it was stardust falling from the sun untold millennia ago whose atoms and molecules evolved into the intricate marvel that is the natural world, with all its wildness, order and beauty; and then into the mystery of embodied spirits like us with a haunting sense of God. What are simpler than the words 'I love you'? Or more mysterious than the transfigured eyes of two people in love? What is more mundane than home-making, or more rewarding than the exploration of another's mystery over a lifetime of marriage? Similarly, could anything be more accessible than a baby in a manger, or a man speaking of justice and God's forgiveness and compassion; or the breaking of bread in a shared meal? What is easier to describe than a cruel and undeserved public death, or an empty grave? What more homely than Peter's decision to return to his fishing? Yet look deeper, and words hesitate and stumble and collapse. Indeed, we should have no words to describe God unless (in those five monosyllables that contain the deepest mystery of all) 'the Word was made flesh'. There is no adequate language to explain the meaning of the Cross, the Easter appearances of the risen Christ (which include breakfast on the sea-shore), the work of the Spirit, the nature of the eucharist, or the new life of the Kingdom. Yet here we are, we preachers (so well described by Paul as 'stewards of the mysteries') daring to stand in pulpits and struggling to speak of these hidden realities; struggling to convey the reality of a world new-made at Easter and potentially transfigured by the grace and goodness of God.

Many seek their firm ground by reducing the mystery and resorting to a safe form of fundamentalism. 'Give me a simple faith,' they say, 'just the facts in black and white'. Yet for most of us life isn't like that, and faith isn't that simple, not if we're seeking truths to live by which will satisfy both mind and heart, and not rightly be written off as foolishly naive by intelligent agnostics and atheists. Faith is a seeking after truth and will always lie somewhere between doubt and certainty, and needs to address that ultimate and most mysterious reality of all: death. Death, which in the words of the poet Isaac Rosenberg in the First World War trenches, can 'drop from the dark/ As easily as song'. As it did so swiftly and violently for him, and as it will do for each of us; and all too soon.

Yet we meet in Eastertide, and sometimes call ourselves 'the Easter people', those who live in the light of the Resurrection. What does it mean to live in the light of that mystery? For me it means believing that God is not a God of the dead but of the living, and trusting that my relationship with the loving, compassionate, forgiving God revealed in Jesus Christ is one that may be *changed* but will not be *ended* by my death. It means trusting that God in his creative power – and in a way I can't begin to imagine – will refashion me, recreating in me everything that has made me my unique self. I have two grounds for such a hope: the first relates to our *incompleteness*, the second to the events of *Easter*.

What do I mean by our 'incompleteness'? I mean our hunger for that truth and beauty of which in this life we have undeniable glimpses, but which just elude our grasp; and our compelling need to find in our lives purpose and mean-ing. St Paul puts his finger on it when he writes of how 'we see through a glass darkly', of how even now 'we know in part', that what we know is persuasive, even if indistinct. And T.S. Eliot talks about those 'hints and guesses' which are all we have by which to plot our human journey. And it is those 'hints and guesses' that we come to church to explore and celebrate. For the *'hints'* are contained in that seductive story of the birth, life, death and resurrection of a man like us, and they've been sufficient to have seized and changed the civi-lised world. And the *'guesses'*? The 'guesses' start with the belief that this man was indeed the unique (though not the exhaustive) revelation of God, and they've been persuasively tested in generation after generation of changed lives. There's a lovely phrase in the funeral service of the Orthodox church in which the priest prays that the departed may have achieved their 'desired homeland'. For the only truth that makes sense of our search for love, and our restless yearning for what is true and good and beautiful, and a resolution of the discords in our lives, is that we are made for life with God and are dissatisfied and incomplete until we rest in him. He is our homeland: at once the ground of our deepest experiences of being loved and forgiven, the *source* of every intimation of beauty and each moment of insight, of every stirring of compassion or anger at injustice, and it's these things which stamp us as being made in his likeness. He is not only their *ground*: he is also their *fulfilment*; and to hope for heaven is to set our hunger in the context of that new quality of life which is called 'eternal'. Life measured as we measure our deepest relationships, not in terms of days or years, but in terms of a deepening love and trust; and this relationship with God once entered into is binding and unbreakable.

How simple these events are! A baby in a manger; a man demonstrating in his life the meaning of self-giving love; this same man hanging on a cross; a garden, an empty grave and one mistaken for the gardener; an invitation to a breakfast of bread and fish by the lakeside. And, after breakfast, the question to Peter which contains both his forgiveness and his task: 'Do you love me? Then follow me.' How simple! In one sense, a child can understand these stories. And yet, because at a different level they claim to reveal once-and-for-all-time the true nature of God and our relationship with him, how deeply mysterious! We can indeed only understand it 'in part'. Yet what is undeniable is that without the Easter experience – however we interpret it – we shouldn't be here. If nothing followed the crucifixion but the sealing of the tomb, there would be no gospel, no commission to Peter, and no church.

The God in whom we believe has the power to create and re-create. At certain critical points in the process of evolution new forms of life have emerged, each with new potential, as infinitely slowly the true nature of our Creator is discerned, until in the person of Jesus something quite new occurs. In short: Easter witnesses to God inaugurating *a new stage in creation*. In Jesus we discern a way of living which can become fully life with God, not only here and now, but eternally, beyond the threshold of death; and in Jesus' life and death and resurrection our own life and death are redefined. So we stand, we Easter people, with (as it were) one foot in time and one foot in eternity, for it is in the risen Christ that we catch the scent of who God truly is and what we are created to be.

21

Not Then But Now

ASCENSION DAY 1999

St Martin-in-the-Fields Church, London

My life is defined by four days: September 10th and October 13th 1929; June 1st 1958; October 16th 1965. Four days on which life went on its ordinary way, and people dug their gardens, and played football, and listened to the radio and washed the dishes. Not knowing that for me they were astonishing, life-changing days, the effects of which have touched every subsequent day of my life. For on the first I was born and entered, protesting, a world whose beauty would amaze and ravish me, and will do so to the end of my life; on the second of those days I was baptised and made a Christian; on the third, hesitant and unsure, yet knowing I could do no other, I was made a priest; and on the fourth I was married, and began a relationship with my wife and then with my children which has enriched my life every day since.

Now all these events happened to me once, at a precise moment on a particular day long since buried in the past. Yet for me they are not just past history. They are not *then* events but *now* events. Each contains within it a truth which I daily enter into afresh. They are about what it means to be me. And each of you will be able to name equivalent days in your past which have shaped your journey and determined what it now means to be you.

Now to be a Christian is to place your own story within the context of four days in another, much greater story: four equally ordinary days when life also went on its familiar way and people went about their daily business, days which have also been despatched to the history books; days, nevertheless, which speak of events that have lost none of their power to shape and change our lives. The first we call Christmas, the second Good Friday, the third Easter Day, the fourth Ascension Day. Each tells of an event as ordinary and extraordinary, as plain and as mysterious, as a birth, a life, a death and a rising.

Four days: four stories, each containing a profound and mysterious truth. The truth of Christmas is that God in Christ himself enters our ordinary world, which is also his world, and shows that he is with us and by our side. The truth of Good Friday is that God in Christ reveals the extent of his love by making himself vulnerable, and is at one with us in all the mess and muddle of human suffering, the victim of injustice and a painful death. The truth of Easter centres on the creative power of God, that creative power I so casually take for granted in every folded leaf and distant star, in every cell in this genetic miracle I call my body. What God does in raising Christ from the dead is as powerful a creative act as that with which over long aeons he first called the world into being, and neither life nor death can ever look the same again.

But what of the fourth day, Ascension Day? What radical truth are those who had known him seeking to convey in this strange story of an airborne Jesus and a cloud and two figures dressed in white? Simply this. That having been with him, watched him, heard his words, witnessed his death, and once again known his presence alive in their midst, they have come to see that *he is a necessary part of any true idea of God*. They could no longer speak of God and not speak of his Christlikeness. What are they telling us? Just that – but it is everything.

And so they begin to use a kind of shorthand that pulls together all the stories – his birth and life and death and rising: the phrase 'Jesus is Lord'. In Paul's words: 'God has highly exalted him, and given him a name which is above every name; that at the name of Jesus every knee should bow ... 'They are saying that Christ's claim upon us is total, that there is no part of the universe that in the end is not to come under his sovereignty. It meant that the standards and values by which his followers seek to live, in both their public and private lives, are his unchanging values of love and forgiveness, justice and mercy, compassion and generosity of spirit.

It still does. To build your life on Christ's values is hard enough, but we are judged, not on whether we succeed, but on whether we deeply desire to do so and are not deterred by repeated failure.

What does it mean to have a vision of what that means for your life, and much more, for the life of your community and nation, and for the worldwide family of nations? It means a stubborn and persistent refusal to conform to worldly values because you have in Christ glimpsed something different: the possibility of a restored and recreated humanity which some call the Kingdom of God.

Is that cloud-cuckoo land? In a world where horror piles on horror, where fundamental human rights are denied, and where nations get rich selling weapons of war, the cynical will think so. Yet there has always been a kind of foolishness about the gospel which says that the world is more subtle than that, and that there is another dimension where God is at work in his people; that no day passes when evil or suffering are not redeemed by countless small acts of love and courage and goodness and self-sacrifice. Set against the intolerable anguish of the Kosovar refugees is the selfless humanitarian work of relief. In the darkest times of Hitler's Third Reich, or Stalin's purges, or in the long night of racial segregation in South Africa or the United States, in the face of torture, abuse and oppression, the human spirit stubbornly refuses to be suppressed, and there is the powerful witness of a minority who, even in prison cells, 'set their minds on

God's Kingdom and his justice above everything else'. Consciously or unconsciously, they witness to the sovereignty of Christ, the ultimate triumph of his way of love over every other force in the world.

So Ascensiontide sets before us an immodest kind of agenda. One that would have been stillborn had it not been for the readiness of those first Christians, in their first glimmering recognition of what God was doing in Christ, to wait in the city for a fifth day. The fifth great day in the Christian calendar that we call the day of Pentecost, when they knew that Christ had kept his word. That he was once again among them, and also within them, but now as a life-giving spirit.

When I was young I chose to bet my life on the truths of which those five stories speak, and stand with those who for two thousand years and in every nation under heaven have placed their trust in the Lordship of Christ. Now that I am old I understand rather better that such truths ultimately lie on the other side of speech, and if you try to pin down the deepest reality in words, you will ultimately fail. For such mysteries begin and end in stillness and silence. And they are nurtured by wonder.

22

Alive and Active

PENTECOST SUNDAY 1989

Westminster Abbey

The other day I found myself sharing a pedestrian crossing in Kensington with an enchanting twelve-foot high dinosaur. It walked slowly up the steps of the Science Museum and through its swing doors, for all the world as if it was going home. It wasn't, of course. Only the out-of-work actor would do that once he had put aside the make-believe of his costume.

There is all the difference in the world between a museum and a home. A museum is fascinating as the record of how past ages have lived and thought, of what has inspired them, of what they felt to be of value. But it is not a place in which you actually choose to live. For a home is a place where relationships are forged: even though you may be surrounded by antique furniture, it is where you are *now*, in your day-to-day living. It's a place where love can grow and people can grow and change as they experience the life and spirit of the family to which they belong.

Some people see this Abbey as a museum, stuffed with historic monuments and filled with antique canons. They could not be more wrong. For it is, of course, like every other church in Christendom, a place in which people meet to worship the God for whom the Middle Ages and the 20th century are all one, the God who is to be met in this present moment or not at all.

Now today is Pentecost and were it not for the Holy Spirit Christianity would be as dead as the dinosaur, and in place of churches we would only have museums. Rather like those former monasteries which Stalin made into museums in Moscow.

And what happened? What happened is one of the more dramatic examples of how the Holy Spirit works. For the Holy Spirit is the Spirit of Jesus Christ alive and active among his followers, the mode in which his presence is now known to us. And no political system, no dictator, could quench the Spirit of Jesus as that claimed the loyalties of the Russian people; so that today the Church flourishes and churches long closed are being re-opened.

Those who wrote the Gospels and the Letters of the New Testament, long after the events of that first Pentecost created the Christian Church, were concerned to demonstrate the way in which Christ's presence is now to be known. At the Last Supper Jesus had spoken of the Spirit who would come upon them, as unpredictable and as powerful as wind or fire, who would continue to open their eyes to the truth and empower them with a strength not their own when he was no longer with them. To believe in the Holy Spirit is to claim that our belief in God, and our own response to Jesus Christ, is an ongoing, changing and developing response to his grace.

By all the laws of cultural and historical change, Jesus ought to mean less and less to fewer and fewer people. Yet in fact he strikes more and more in each generation and in ever-new cultures and societies as the one who has the words of life. It isn't that his words and actions mean exactly the same to us as they did to those who first saw and heard them. It is precisely because he is *not* a figure fixed in history like Pontius Pilate, but a life-giving Spirit who speaks afresh to our hearts of the Father's love, that his words and actions have this apparently inexhaustible power to take root in us.

And the question, the only really vital question, we need to ask ourselves on the feast of Pentecost is quite simply this: are we open to the Holy Spirit and what he has to teach us now in the midst of our Christian journey? To have met Jesus of Nazareth was no doubt both a comforting *and* a challenging experience: both a reassuring *and* a disruptive one. The same must be true of any real encounter with the Holy Spirit.

Too often we seem anxious about containing the Faith as once and for all revealed. We try to safeguard it by assuming there was a cut-off point – the fourth century, or the Reformation or 1662 – when everything was fixed, like flies in amber. But that is the museum principle at work again.

And the whole thrust of the Gospel, the whole excitement of the work of the Spirit, is that there is a continuing revelation of God in every age as men and women genuinely seek to be open to him. Jesus promised that the Spirit would lead us into all truth. It isn't that the central truths change: it is that those truths need to be understood, interpreted and communicated to every new generation afresh. The question is how those truths are to be presented and the values and authority of Jesus Christ affirmed when confronted with the moral dilemmas as well as the social and technological revolution of our own time.

How today do we learn how best to speak the universal language of love? Only by God's grace. Only by waiting on the Spirit. Only by being genuinely open to what God may be revealing of himself in the new issues of the 1980s – for example, that of women priests.

Through the Holy Spirit we who are Christians speak with different tongues but we speak a common language. We know the world as God's world. We speak of him as Abba, Father, one we can trust. We acknowledge the authority of Jesus as Lord. We belong to one body of Christ. We find him in the breaking of the bread. We know ourselves and each other as often wilfully sinful, but redeemed, forgiven, loved and valued by God. And so we are set free, if we will, to speak the language of love.

I have come to value, almost above all other prayers, the collect in the new Prayer Book that we say each morning in St Faith's Chapel at the end of morning prayer. It is a collect which stands with the best written in any age.

> Eternal God and Father,
> you create us by your power
> and redeem us by your love.
> Guide and strengthen us by your Spirit
> that we may give ourselves in love and service
> to one another and to you.

And that daily prayer is re-echoed in that other prayer we say at the end of every Eucharist, when we ask God not just to send us out, but to send us out 'in the power of your Spirit to live and work to your power and glory.'

To say either prayer with conviction is to ask for that openness to the Spirit which is the only proper response of a faith which speaks not of a religious museum but of a family and of a pilgrimage.

23

At Any and Every Moment

PENTECOST 1997

Corpus Christi College Chapel, Cambridge

The term card reveals that I came up to Corpus in 1951. Winston Churchill was Prime Minister, sweets were still rationed, and Tony Blair was not even a twinkle in his father's eye. And I think of the thousands of words that washed over me Sunday by Sunday as I sat in this chapel, of which I cannot now remember a single one.

Yet words matter. The poet Seamus Heaney writes of the profound effect the words of another Irish poet, Patrick Kavanagh, once had on him as a young man. 'He took my familiar (childhood) world' he writes, 'and embodied it in new-minted words. Here was the stillness and heat and solitude of the sunlit fields, the inexplicable melancholy of distant work-sounds, all caught in a language that was familiar yet strangely new ... All at once I knew the primitive delight of *world become word.*'

And is it not extraordinary that the loveliest poetry ever written, the most powerful drama, the wisdom of the philosophers and the holiness of the saints has come down to us clothed in the 26 letters of the alphabet? From this handful of letters Shakespeare creates Lear and Othello, Milton creates *Paradise Lost*, Dante the *Divine Comedy*. For words are the only mould we have into which our innermost thoughts must be pressed if we are to share them. Fragile, imprecise, slippery words in which an invisible thought, a sudden idea, must be embodied, incarnated, given substance. They are all I have

82

with which just to pass the time of day, or to make a declaration of love that will change my life for ever, or with which to share an insight about the Mystery.

Now I have a weakness for second-hand bookshops, but I tend to avoid the sections labelled 'second-hand theology', for most of it is just that – second-, third-, even fourth-hand: people's ideas about other people's ideas about God. Instead I make for the poets and the novelists, for they know that words must come new-minted and from the heart; and they employ telling images and metaphors that hint at deeper meanings as they try and capture a little of the mystery of what it is to be human. They take the a and the b and the c and juggle them so skilfully that in telling their story they seem to be telling ours too; some of the more perceptive of them discerning in what happens in our lives the sound of God's voice and the movement of God's spirit.

Now these could be mere words on my part, empty words strung together as I sit in my study down in Salisbury trying to think myself into the ambience of Corpus Chapel on a Sunday evening in May with the Tripos just round the corner. But in fact they're not: they come from the heart. And if I wanted to try and convince you of that, I might add: 'I give you my word'. Not just in the obvious sense of: 'You can trust me', but in a subtler and much more profound sense too. For in saying, 'I give you my word' I am saying, 'I want to take something that is part of me – an idea, a belief – and flesh it out in words that may strike a chord in your own minds and hearts.' So they've got to be true words, speaking of what we share as human beings.

That is to say: unless I give you something of myself, words that come from my own centre and which I've felt and tested on my own pulse, and unless in return you give me something of yourself, your attention, we remain strangers and there will have been no real communication – just a small disturbance in the air, as if a flight of birds had passed overhead on their way to roost elsewhere.

83

Now if that is true of us, it must also be true of the God in whose image we are made. He wants to give us his word, to communicate to us something of his own inner nature, so that we begin to glimpse what he is like. And isn't the whole Bible about God giving us his Word, choosing the *a* and the *b* and the *c* of ordinary lives and ordinary events to communicate his word to his creation?

So the book Genesis describes a God who out of a profound silence says: 'Let there be light'. And as chaos gives way to order, as God sings the creation into being, his Word is discerned in the unfolding panorama of a universe of awesome power, and then of such beauty as to ravish the senses. 'I give you my word' says God as civilisations rise and fall, until eventually there emerges a particular nation, Israel, and within that nation particular men who are responsive to his word, and often at great cost proclaim it. But the words fall on deaf ears and in a new and spectacular way God says: 'I give you my Word: I give you myself.' And so St John, bringing to the birth of Jesus the deep insight of the poet, says not 'Once upon a time a baby was born', but 'The Word made flesh and dwelt among us, full of grace and truth'. Here is nothing less than the earthing of God in his creation, so that from this moment everything has to be redefined. Everything, starting with God. A God who in Jesus is saying: 'But I am not like *that*: I am like *this*!' God revealed as Christlike.

Here, then, in what we call Christmas and Passiontide and Easter, is God's definitive Word to us about who he is and who we are and could be. Here is God speaking our language, living our life and dying our death.

Yet that's only half the story, for that was *once* and *then*, not here and now. Which is why the real beginning of the Christian story is not Christmas or Easter, or even Ascension Day, but Whitsun, the day of Pentecost. For Pentecost changes everything. Pentecost says: 'The Word that was once made flesh and seen in Jesus Christ is now made Spirit, and let loose in all the world.' Pentecost says: 'If you would encounter Christ you must do so in the moment that is now or not at all'; that unless you see the Christlike God in the next person you meet, there is no point in looking for him further.

See in your mind two matching pictures, the old creation and the new. In his first creation God breathes his life, his spirit, into the nostrils of Adam. In the second picture, the risen Christ breathes on his disciples in the upper room and says: 'Receive the Holy Spirit', and that is the new creation, the creation of the community of those in every age who will choose to be open to the spirit of Jesus Christ. For Christ has no body in the world other than those who choose to live in his spirit. So the Word that was once made flesh is now made Spirit. Which sounds like a nifty piece of preacher's gobblede-gook. What does it actually mean?

It means that Jesus Christ is not some inspired but remote figure in the past whom Christians meet to remember, but one who may be encountered at any and every moment of our lives, one who speaks directly to our hearts and whose Spirit is able to shape us (if that is our desire) in the profound-est ways. It means that only when that deepest part of me that I call my spirit is open to God's Spirit am I able to see with new eyes. See God as he really is in the light Jesus throws upon him as my loving Father. See people as they really are in the light Jesus throws upon them as my brothers and sisters. Only then do I begin to be disturbed and haunted by and come to share Jesus' concept of 'the Kingdom', that commu-nity based on justice and equity, people who know the liberating power of forgiveness and the healing power of love. And infinitely slowly, and gradually over a lifetime, I begin if I truly desire it to be drawn by the Spirit into that enviable relationship Jesus had with the Father and with all whom he met: one of trust and thankfulness, compassion and generous love.

And so tonight I think back to the thousands of words that washed over me nearly 50 years ago as I sat in this chapel, and

85

I cannot remember a single one. And now I've added, my computer tells me, 1500 more, which you in your turn will quickly forget. And yet ... and yet ... in the end it wasn't the words. It was the *spirit* in which *some* of those words were spoken that touched me and fed my spirit and helped to form me on my human journey – which has turned out to be a journey with God as its goal.

And what I really need to say on this feast of Pentecost, as I touch base at Corpus again after a lifetime, is that it was in this Chapel that I first began as an adult to understand something of what it might mean to be open to the Spirit; to speak of God as 'Abba, Father'; and to belong to the Spirit-filled community. It was here that, in certain people and certain actions, I caught glimpses of that Christlike life that can only be the work of God the Holy Spirit. And if you press my further I can only add: 'I cannot tell what it will be like for you. I can only speak of what I have seen and what I know. And give you my word'.

24

Christ and Healing

ST LUKE'S DAY 1989

Westminster Abbey

Today is St Luke's Day and St Luke, by tradition, was not only the writer of the third Gospel and the Book of Acts, but a doctor. And the collect for today speaks of Luke the physician proclaiming the love and healing power of Jesus Christ. And so I want to talk to you about Christ and healing.

In the north quire aisle of the Abbey there is a marble bust of Joseph Lister, the Victorian surgeon who was the pioneer of antiseptic treatment and particularly of the prevention of death resulting from operations.

How amazed Lister would have been if he could have known even a small part of the advances in medicine in our time. I think of the work in genetics and immunology, of organ and heart transplants, of what is called micro-surgery, of the use of laser beams in the treatment of cancer. And yet I can't help wondering if in another hundred years as significant a break-through in the treatment of damaged human beings may be seen as the work of Freud and Jung and their followers on the dynamics of the mind, and their perception of the mysterious complexity of a human being – of how body and mind and spirit are inter-related in the unity which is you.

No doubt that story I read just now of the four men opening up the roof and lowering their paralysed friend's body at the feet of Jesus has always spoken powerfully of the need to be forgiven, and so healed inwardly in spirit as well as in body, but our knowledge today that very much illness is psychosomatic brings such an incident into even sharper focus. Of course it was once all too natural to believe your sickness, or any other disaster that befell you, was sent by God, certainly as a test and probably as a punishment. Today we know that sickness may have causes which are far more complex. Because the body affects the mind and the mind the body, a sudden shock – perhaps a bereavement – can set off a physical illness. Or perhaps we consistently over-eat or over-drink, or smoke too much, and physical damage is done. We may even kill ourselves. And we may dimly see that John's asthma, or Dick's ulcer, or Mary's arthritis or hiatus hernia, aren't just chance happenings, sent out of the blue, but relate to some fear or anxiety, or anger or guilt or the struggle to survive in a competitive world.

Any talk, then, of sickness and healing is full of ambiguities. Is the sickness in the body or the mind? Does it need surgery, drugs, prayer, the laying on of hands – or simply a sympathetic listening ear? What is health? There is the paradox – and we can all think of examples – of the man with multiple sclerosis who seems a more whole and complete human being than his neighbour who has never had a day's illness yet who seems quite unaware of the deeper meaning of life. Or the woman whose illness itself looks like a headlong flight from life and its demands. And then there are those who discover themselves and maybe discover God in any real sense for the first time in the dark night of sickness and suffering. And there is the huge paradox of why some people are physically healed while others are not.

Now I don't believe you can answer any of these questions until you have asked the prior question: what is life for? Is it for happiness? Happiness in the sense of the satisfying of one want after another? If so, then for most people it really is the worst of all possible worlds.

But perhaps that is not what life is for. Jesus knew more clearly than any of us that life can be unfair, painful and short: that the good do often contract terminal diseases, that the worldly do often prosper and live to a ripe old age. And yet he never doubted the power or the justice or the love of God. When sick people came to him he dealt with them with compassion. Some he healed. But he didn't *explain* sickness or suffering or even look to God to explain them. He simply said that God is to be trusted. I am to have faith that in sickness as in health God loves me, he is my Father, and his desire for me is that I learn to trust him (in Job's words) 'even though he slay me'. Only then shall I find that inner wholeness and tranquillity which is not thwarted by a damaged body.

What I am saying is that I don't understand any more than anyone else why Peter dies of leukaemia at the age of eighteen. But although God has given us the skill to explore the nature of the cancer cell so that the day may come when leukaemia is defeated, he doesn't expect me to understand the mystery, the WHY of the cancer cell. He asks me to trust him. And for a Christian the answer to the question: what is life for? is this. Life is the setting *in which we learn how to trust and how to love*. How to trust and how to love both God and each other, and so discover what such trust and love can do when you seek to make them the basis of your life.

Sickness, then, is potentially a destructive process which can be made into a creative one, for it can be a time to find God in darkness as well as light. And once you accept that possibility, the possibility that sickness can be redeemed depending on how you respond to it, then the world begins to look as if it has been made for learning and practising trust and love; indeed, that it is the best of all possible worlds in which to do so.

Now none of that implies that sickness is something to which we should be resigned. Jesus saw disease as something to be fought. He is God's healing power made flesh, his healing actions part of what St Paul calls the 'kindness and love of God our saviour for mankind'; and it is now part of the mission of the Church to heal sick bodies as well as sick minds. And I believe we are only on the brink of discovering how to use the natural power of healing many people possess, or how, as doctors or priests or counsellors, we can address the whole person in his or her need for reconciliation, for forgiveness and reassurance as well, perhaps, as surgery or pills. One of the lessons of the charismatic movement has been to remind us that those who take prayer and healing seriously and make large requests often see results which put our timid faith to shame.

And yet I am sometimes bothered by the assumption of enthusiastic Christians that if those who are sick only had sufficient faith they would invariably be healed physically. For that is not only nonsense, it is cruel nonsense. For what the Gospel offers us is not eternal health – how could it, for we all have to die – but eternal life: by which it means a quality of relationship with God in Jesus Christ which no physical infirmity can destroy. And it is that kind of confidence and hope in God which is the real inward healing of the human spirit. That is why Jesus sought out sinners even more than he sought out the sick, and why 'son, your sins are forgiven' precedes 'arise, take up your bed and walk' in that story of the young man, for Jesus knew that true healing is inseparable from that restoration of forgiveness and trust which have such a profound effect on the body and its diseases.

So the ministry of healing continues. We surround the sick with prayer and love, helping them to that expectant trust in God. But avoiding any sweeping claims about perfect bodily health which can be distressing. For there remains the mystery of pain and sickness even in the most saintly people. And you come to understand that hand in hand with the ministry of healing goes what I can only call a ministry of *suffering*: people who by the sheer quality of their lives prove that no virus, no cancer cell, can in the end frustrate the purpose of God. His purpose is that each of us shall so grow in trust and love that we attain the wholeness for which he made us, that relationship which no disease, no process of ageing, and not even death can destroy.

25

The Wholesome Medicine of the Gospel

ST LUKE'S DAY 1998

St Thomas Church, Fifth Avenue, New York

The opening and closing words of tonight's first lesson from Isaiah:

> How beautiful on the mountains are the feet of the herald, the bringer of good news ... (for) the whole world from end to end shall see the deliverance wrought by our God.
> What good news? What deliverance? Nothing less than the healing of humankind.

It was in 1823 that Charles Mackintosh invented the waterproof, the Monroe doctrine finally stopped Britain or any other European power from colonising in the United States, James Fennimore Cooper wrote *The Pioneers*, and the first St Thomas church was founded on Houston Street. Later, you moved to Fifth Avenue and lost everything in a devastating fire, but by 1912 were resurrected, phoenix-like, in this numinous, peaceful building that it is a joy to return to once again. But neither St Thomas, nor Westminster Abbey, nor any other church in the world would exist were it not for one who once, uniquely, looked into the ultimate mystery, the source and sustainer of this astonishing (if unpredictable) universe and said that his name is Father and his nature Love.

It is, of course, the unpredictability that hurts: the confusing mix of wonder and dread, of beauty and pain, love and grief; but also the perplexing mix of good and bad, creative and destructive that lies deep within the human heart. And the Christian faith has an utterly realistic understanding of the darkness, both of sin and sickness. We know that the first may lead to crucifixion or its equivalent in the battlefields and torture chambers and prison cells around the world; and the second to a body disfigured and damaged, or a life cut short by mortal illness. And yet the Christian faith affirms truths that go deeper and are more powerful. In the Book of Common Prayer the collect for St Luke's Day speaks of Luke as a 'physician of the soul' and of the 'wholesome medicine' of the Gospel; and it is of that 'wholesome medicine', of the Gospel's power to love and heal, that I would speak.

There are in the Gospels forty stories of Jesus healing. And if you analyse them you discover that (with very few exceptions) those who are healed are the poor, the voiceless, the marginalised and those who are despised within society. Jesus rejects the current thought that sickness is the result of sin. But his healing goes far beyond physical changes in one who is sick. In almost every case the person who is healed is socially or politically or religiously disadvantaged, unloved or unnoticed by the majority of those around them. He embraces those whom few in his day would consider touching: the leper, the mad, the blind and lame, the adulterous and immoral, and those of other faiths.

Zacchaeus, for example, is demonised by a hostile crowd because of an unfair tax, and Jesus restores to him his place within the community and his relationship with his neighbours; others are forgiven even before they confess their sin. Jesus recognises the complex nature of each person, the way our minds and bodies and spirits inter-relate – so that he says to the paralytic man let down through the roof by his friends 'Your sins are forgiven' before he says 'take up your bed and walk', knowing that the peace of mind which forgiveness brings is an inseparable part of healing.

It was Martin Luther who wrote that 'Christ's proper work is to declare the grace of God, to console and to enliven'. Jesus never explained sickness: he simply affirmed, in the way he lived his life and the way he met his death, that God is to be trusted. So that the Gospel healings are above all actions which tell of the love of God for the forsaken and seemingly damned, especially those who are excluded on religious or moral grounds.

I have touched on one other extraordinary departure on Jesus' part from all accepted religious protocol. Not only can we never earn that forgiveness which is God's free and gracious gift, but Jesus seems to assure sinners of forgiveness before they ask for it or express their penitence. Look at the parable of the Prodigal Son, where the father watches and waits and then *runs* to embrace his returning child; or the story of the woman at Simon's house who anoints Jesus' feet. It is as if the Gospels are saying that you can only truly confess in response to the grace of God's forgiveness. Which is all of a piece with the great affirmation of the New Testament that 'we love because God first loves us'. That faith and trust which are so central to our healing are our answer to God revealing his true nature in Jesus Christ. Revealing himself in a life which from first to last defines God's love and forgiveness, showing them to be the most powerful forces in the world.

When I look back at my ten years at Westminster Abbey, the events that are burned into my memory are all healing events. I think of one Good Friday. A large wooden cross had been made by a carpenter in Belfast. It was carried through the streets of Westminster from the Roman Catholic Cathedral to the Abbey, accompanied by nearly 1,000 people. In the nave an Irish Roman Catholic, a member of the Church of Ireland and a Presbyterian all spoke of their shame and their penitence, and asked on behalf of their communities for

94

forgiveness. We sang a Good Friday hymn and shared the peace; and that Good Friday there was healing.

I think of a televised service at the outbreak of the Gulf War during the course of which a senior Muslim leader and a senior Jewish rabbi read alternative verses of the 23rd Psalm, and at the end of it clasped hands and embraced in a symbolic act of healing and reconciliation. And I recall the service to mark the 50th anniversary of the end of the war with Japan, in which the old soldiers who had suffered terribly in prisoner-of-war camps joined many Japanese with whom over the years they have worked, often at great cost, for reconciliation; and Japanese, British and American children placed paper cranes on the Grave of the Unknown Warrior – as they do on war graves in Japan. There was forgiveness and the healing of memories in that joint service, and at the door afterwards many were in tears.

So then: by touching and embracing the afflicted and the outcast Jesus is doing something radically new. He is challenging the crowds and onlookers to consider their implicit or explicit role in that person's suffering. And he is affirming those he encounters with the assurance of God's forgiveness. But there is one further dimension to his healing acts. For in some strange sense Jesus actually takes on the suffering and affliction of those he cures. It becomes part of him. By dining with Zacchaeus, by consorting with sinners, by inviting women of ill repute into his company, he risks being misunderstood and ostracised. It is as if in his compassion he takes on their brokenness, until eventually on the cross Jesus is himself broken, the outcast, ostracised and abused.

And this, we claim, this crucified figure with words of forgiveness of his lips and his love unbroken, is the most accurate picture of God the world has ever seen. Which is why I want to end by speaking of what felt to me like the Abbey's most significant piece of ministry, and one for which we were sometimes criticised. In 1988, when the AIDS virus was making its first real impact on London, the churches by and large didn't want to know. We had a new group of outcasts in our midst. And so for ten years I invited three times a year to the Abbey's medieval Jerusalem Chamber groups of some fifty people, many with full-blown AIDS, some who worked in AIDS hospices. We had a leisurely buffet supper, and then I would take them on a night tour of the Abbey, ending with brief prayers and a shared silence in one of the chapels. Few of them were churchgoers and often expressed surprise and gratitude that a church at the heart of the British establishment was concerned with people who are sick and in need. Concerned to show that the church's role is to be a non-judgmental, caring body in the face of human suffering, however that suffering has come about.

I know that those who came for eight years to those AIDS evenings went away, in Luther's words, 'consoled and enlivened'; or, as we might put it, affirmed. Sick as they remained, there had been a kind of healing. And not only did we affirm them: they affirmed us. And I knew that, out of the whole varied range of the Abbey's worship, life and ministry, nothing was closer to the heart of the healing, reconciling, affirming God whose name is Father and whose nature is love.

26

People Like Us

ALL SAINTS' DAY 1996

St Margaret's Church, Westminster

Last year, when the Abbey's Lady Chapel (Henry VII's Chapel) was being restored there was scaffolding up to the roof and it was possible to examine at close range the ninety-five saints, each on their stone pedestal, who surround it. They are vigorous masterpieces of the early sixteenth century, and the last on the south aisle is your patron saint, Margaret of Antioch, with a cross in her hand and her foot resting on the head of a rather Disney-like grinning dragon. They make strange bed-fellows, those whom we are celebrating this weekend, the saints, martyrs and confessors of the Church. Beside St Margaret in the Abbey is St Dunstan holding the devil's nose with a pair of tongs, St Anthony with his pig and St Roche with his dog; St Anne, teaching the Virgin Mary to read; a bespectacled St Philip; St Martin, giving alms to a beggar with wooden legs; and poor St Uncumber, who didn't want to marry the King of Sicily, prayed for a miracle, and found she had grown a beard overnight, which was no doubt not quite what she had in mind but proved remarkably effective. They seem, these saints, both familiar and remote: familiar because they are so full of character, like a group of Chaucer's pilgrims on the way to Canterbury, but as remote as those Moonlike haloes that serve as their holy hats. And at All Saints-tide we should be thinking of real, flesh-and-blood people, not medieval statues, however appealing.

So let's start somewhere else. Not with haloes but with what the halo represents. And I don't mean a kind of unctuous piety. When the monk Thomas Merton told the story of his Christian journey he described a profoundly illuminating disclosure in the unlikeliest place: on the corner of a busy street in Louisville, Kentucky:

> I was suddenly overwhelmed (he writes) with the realization that I loved all these people, that we could not be alien to one another, even though we were total strangers. It was like waking from a dream of separateness ... to take your place as a member of the human race. I had the immense joy of being human, a member of the race in which God himself became incarnate. If only everybody could realize this. But it cannot be explained. There is no way of telling people that they are all walking around shining like the sun.

When they asked the painter Van Gogh why he painted as he did he said it was because he wanted to show that human beings had something of the eternal about them. He wrote: 'I want to paint people with that something of the eternal which the halo used to symbolize, and which I seek to convey by the radiance and vibration of my colouring', and indeed, if you look at some of his portraits, there is a kind of rainbow of light around the head.

Now here is the paradox: that we human beings have immortal yearnings, and yet end up as a handful of dust. Or do we? Physically, yes of course we do. But we are not just flesh and blood. Dust we may be, but it's a dust imbued with that restless, searching, creative, imaginative spirit that we call soul. We are each of us an embodied spirit, who dreams of a destiny beyond our imagining in the nearer presence of God. Which of us hasn't experienced moments when we know beyond question that the petty nature of so much of the give-and-take of our daily lives is not what life is truly for, and that our deeper happiness and our ultimate fulfilment lie in words like hope and trust and wonder, forgiveness and compassion, and the give-and-take of an unselfish love. We know that there are times when the darkness of life seems overwhelming; but are not many of us here at this Eucharist because of a hope and a light to be found even in the darkest places? Because we believe in the Christ-like God who was once made in our likeness and shared our pain and died our death, since when they look quite different.

So who are the saints? Not many of them are stuck on stone pedestals or in the corners of medieval stained-glass windows, as remote as their haloes. For saints are those who, looking at Jesus Christ, see in him both the human face of God and the truth about their own destiny, and never again seriously doubt it. They don't cease to be human: as fallible, vulnerable, sometimes as aggravating as we all are. But they are those for whom there has been a real disclosure which enables them to see God and themselves and everyone else with new eyes, and they are then committed to the way of love. Or rather, they *desire* to be, for it's a long and difficult journey, and all that God asks of us is our desire, not our achievement.

And I believe that, if you are anything like me, your own Christian faith will have been validated not by written creeds or theological books, but by glimpsing, in this man or that woman you have known something of that loving, Christ-like spirit: perhaps by examples of courage and trust in the face of illness or dying, or by acts of forgiveness and compassion which are in startling contrast to what comes more naturally to most of us most of the time.

But why do I keep on speaking of saints as 'them'? Why not 'us'? For St Paul always addresses those to whom he is writing in the young churches as 'saints'. For him a saint is simply a sinner who has turned his face in a new direction, someone who is open now to the grace of God, open now to the ever-renewing, forgiving and affirming Spirit of Jesus Christ.

And so, at All Saints-tide, we don't celebrate some remote heavenly House of Lords. We celebrate people like us, people who have been baptized into the body of Christ and who are therefore called to be saints. And if this weekend we are especially remembering and celebrating those who have opened themselves most fully and obviously to the Spirit of Christ, that is simply because they illuminate the words 'human being'. They show us our true potential as men and women made in God's likeness. We affirm them because they affirm us. They point us to our true destiny and they rekindle our hope.

27

His Promise Our Hope

ALL SOULS' DAY 1987

All Saints' Church, Margaret Street, London

Some words from tonight's Gospel: 'It is my Father's will that everyone who looks on the Son and puts his faith in him shall possess eternal life'.

'Men fear death' wrote Francis Bacon, 'as children fear to go in the dark ... (and yet) it is as natural to die as to be born; and to a little infant; perhaps the one is as painful as the other.'

There is a part of us which can glimpse the truth of that: we understand how it is as natural to die as to be born, that death, like birth, is a transformation, a dying to all that is familiar. It is that final surrender of ourselves in trust to God, the climax of all those tiny acts of dying, of the giving and sharing of ourselves with others, of which the Christian life consists.

But it is always a going out into the unknown, into the dark.

And that is precisely what we fear. It is because we don't know and can't imagine how it may be for us 'when the bright day is done and we are for the dark'; and so we are afraid. Afraid of losing control; afraid of the whole process of dying; afraid of the loneliness of that final journey; fearful of being separated from all those we love; of never seeing another spring or another autumn; fearful even – as one eighty-year-old said to me – that there may be no books in heaven.

How then do we cope with the thought of death?

There are some for whom the whole subject is taboo: it is as if by disregarding it, or by using such euphemisms as 'he passed away' or 'he was taken' or 'she has been called home' or even, heaven help us, 'he has gone to meet the great Reaper in the sky', it is as if by such circumlocution death can be kept at bay.

Others trivialize the reality of death by thinking of it as a momentary evil, of little consequence to those who believe in resurrection: a shadow lying across the path to glory. Every cloud has a silver lining and the suffering of Good Friday is quickly reversed and blotted out by the joy of Easter Day.

But that is not the belief of the New Testament, and at All Saints' tide and on All Souls' Day, when we rejoice with all those who have gone before us, those who died in the Resurrection faith and are now alive in Christ Jesus, it is as well to understand the true relationship between life and death, death and eternal life.

Death in the Gospels means Gethsemane: it means the agony and bloody sweat; it means the pain of the scourging, the agony of the Cross, the loneliness of dying. It means the desolation of 'my God, my God – where are you?' And it means the enduring, costly trust at the end of 'Father, into thy hands I commend my spirit'.

Death for each of us will not be like that, but it will still be the most difficult journey we have to make and it may draw out from us every bit of courage, patience and faith that we possess.

Last month I sat beside a friend as he died, after a year-long battle with cancer. It was the most peaceful end you could imagine, a true falling asleep between one breath and the next so that it was hard to catch the precise moment between life and death. But he had not fallen asleep: he had been alive and now he was dead; and within minutes the blood had drained from his face and his limbs quickly became cold as stone. It isn't frightening to see someone die, but it is awe-inspiring: an awe-inspiring glimpse into the mystery of life and death. Everything that was the expression of a unique human being, the familiar flesh, the familiar look or smile or touch, are now no more than Hamlet's 'quintessence of dust'. Every time a man or woman dies it is for those who love them as if a whole world has been extinguished.

'Dust thou art and unto dust shalt thou return'; and each Ash Wednesday, when we kneel to receive on our forehead the imposition of ashes, we have a salutary reminder of that fact.

Yet that is only half the story. For in the final words of the Contakion for the Dead 'All we go down to the dust; And weeping o'er the grave we make our song: *Alleluya*! *Alleluya*! *Alleluya*!'

Dust we may be, but we are dust that dreams of glory, dust that is touched by the spirit and shot through with hope. We have bodies that will die, but we are not simply bodies; we are embodied spirits, created by God for eternal life.

What the New Testament claims is that in Jesus Christ, crucified and risen, the Almighty and creative power of God breaks into history in a new and breath-taking way.

And what the Christian faith proclaims is not that death is insignificant but that it is not the ultimate state: it does not have the final word. Good Friday is not reversed by Easter Day: Good Friday is a day of blood and death, a real and painful death and yet also a victorious death, and on Easter Day God vindicates his Son by raising him to life. The Easter faith, the faith proclaimed at every Eucharist, is not that death is no less real but that it is not final. It is seen not to be the end for which we are created. It has lost its sting. But if we don't understand the reality of death we shall not understand the reality of resurrection.

When Jesus stood among his disciples after his resurrection and said 'Peace be with you' it was for them the final proof that all he had said about trusting God and about the Father's love was true; yet he still bore the marks of the nails in his hands and the mark of the spear in his side.

103

Jesus does not offer us freedom from pain and death. What he offers is eternal life: a new relationship here and now with God, our spirits drawn by his Spirit, a relationship of such a quality that nothing that can happen to us can destroy it. 'Neither life, nor death ... can separate us from the love of God in Christ Jesus our Lord' writes St Paul. And in the words of my text, Jesus says: 'It is my Father's will that everyone who looks on the Son and puts his faith in him shall possess eternal life.'

That is his promise. That is our hope. That is the hope we share with all those who have gone before us on our journey home to God. Because of Good Friday and Easter we know that in the end all shall be well, and that we are held through life and through death by the God who creates and recreates. That is a large claim, but as those who follow Christ and all his saints we dare not settle for anything less.

28

Always and Everywhere

THANKSGIVING DAY (UNITED STATES) 1997

Kanuga Conference Center, Hendersonville, North Carolina

Surely only Albert Gooch could be original enough – or should I say perverse enough? – to invite an *Englishman* to chaplain this most American of weeks, and to preach on this Thanksgiving Day, a day for which there is no British equivalent. And yes, before you rush to put me right, I *do* know that it was those 39 English settlers at Berkeley Plantation, Virginia, who started it all in 1619, but not many other English people know that.

I said 'yes' to Albert for two reasons. My first reason, and my only qualification, is a deep love for the United States and a warm regard for its people. Not only was I brought up on a diet of those classic Hollywood films of the '40s and '50s, but in more recent years I have had a close encounter with a rattlesnake in Texas; I have stood on the South Rim and watched the sun rise over the Grand Canyon, and on the North Rim to see it set; I have been woken at 3 a.m. in Waco by a neighbour shooting armadillos in his yard; I have been hugged protesting by Goofy and Donald Duck in Disney World in L.A.; I have swum in the freezing seas of San Francisco; preached at Harvard balanced on crutches; preached to the Southern Baptist students of Baylor University and survived; marvelled at Mesa Verde and Bryce Canyon; torn a cartilage in the Painted Desert; stayed in the house used in the filming of *On Golden Pond* and heard the loons calling; driven through New Hampshire in the Fall;

collected fossils in the scrublands of Oklahoma; listened to jazz in New Orleans; marvelled at the bluebonnets and Indian paintbrush of a Texan Spring; lost my baggage (twice) at Greenville/Spartanburg; driven in the Blue Ridge Mountains of Virginia; enjoyed the most generous hospitality in the world; and Sunday by Sunday for the last ten glorious years welcomed Americans from every state of your great country to Westminster Abbey. All of which illustrates the first law of public speaking: if you're unsure of your audience, flatter them.

I will tell you my second reason for saying 'yes' to Albert when Alison and I and some of our family were invited to share this week with you – but not right away, for it's a little more subtle, and it starts with a sense of surprise. Surprise that the keeping of Thanksgiving is not getting less, when so much in modern life is opposed to what it stands for. The first Thanksgiving Days were harvest festivals, which is why it still takes place in the fall. Yet we no longer reap the harvest in the old traditional ways. Few town children know what it's like to grow a pumpkin or gather in the hay. More and more we're out of touch with the land and shop in the impersonal, sterile landscape of malls. And Thanksgiving is the great family day, yet we live in an age where there is frequent divorce and large numbers of single parents.

And yet Thanksgiving day is still compelling, and families who may have long ago forgotten its origin and true meaning are drawn together to celebrate at a family meal. As one of you said to me: 'It's even better than Christmas: all the fun, but none of the hassle of buying presents.' (The children might not agree). So why do you make so much of Thanksgiving – and why do I applaud and envy you?

Because deep at its centre this day is about a word, a concept, a vision that human beings can't do without; indeed, it's what makes us human. The word, the concept, the vision, is *community* or *communion* or *company*. Three powerful words with the same meaning. They describe that human need for other people which is so deeply ingrained within us. For we're not just egos, spinning along on our lonely journey to the grave. We're *persons*, but we only become persons in the full sense as we relate in love and friendship with other persons. Which is why Thanksgiving, despite all the hype, the parades and the razzmatazz, centres on taking part in a shared meal with your family, a meal at which the presence of every single member makes a difference. For some it may be a time of nostalgia or sadness, but its abiding value is that it is a time at which the sense of family and the value of each of its members is affirmed.

And that sharing of bread, of course, goes right to the heart both of the Jewish and of the Christian faiths. In Old Testament times it is at once a sign of peace and trust and fellowship. And much more, of forgiveness and reconciliation, for how can you break bread and share a meal with someone against whom you bear a grudge? Inviting a person to a meal is a way of saying: 'I welcome you into my life and the life of my family'. Which is why when Jesus wanted to show beyond any shadow of doubt that God loved sinners he didn't just *say* so. He told social outcasts like Matthew and Zacchaeus that he was coming to dinner with them, and over and over again he spoke of God's Kingdom, that state of life when all will live in peace and equity, as being like a banquet. A shared feast with literally heavenly food and drink, and to which all are invited: men and women and children, black and white, Democrat and Republican, migrant and native-born, rich and poor – for at God's table and in God's sight all those differences that now divide us will be infinitely less important than our membership of that new community that is the Kingdom of God.

And there is something else. For not only did Jesus gather together a company of followers, but on the night before he died he chose one action by which he wanted that company to be identified and united with him in all the future years. He, whom St John calls 'the living bread', chose a thanks-

107

giving meal. For that's what it is, this service that some call Holy Communion and some call the Eucharist. 'Holy *Communion*' because its purpose is to build up the holy *community* of God's people. And '*eucharist*' because that is the Greek word for *thanksgiving*. And since that historic night when Jesus shared bread in the company of his friends, not a single day has gone by, nor will it until the world ends, without groups of Christians somewhere in the world taking bread and wine and breaking the bread and sharing it together, saying as they do so: 'It is right, and a good and joyful thing, always and everywhere to give thanks'. It is right that there is thanksgiving at the very centre of our lives, not just on Thanksgiving Day but on every day of the year.

And so my second reason for gladly saying 'yes' when Albert Gooch invited us to share your Thanksgiving Week, was because of the word 'company'. 'Company' from the two Latin words 'cum' and 'panis' meaning 'to share bread'. It's one of the greatest of words, 'company', and I can't think of a better one to describe Thanksgiving Day. Or to describe what we do at the heart of our family life and indeed of life itself. Or of what lies at the heart of the Christian life, that life that began in the Easter garden and will end in the city of God with that innumerable company of angels and saints.

Those who understand the word 'company' understand that the breaking and sharing of bread, whether in church or out of it, is at once that simplest and most profound affirmation of who and what we are. That it delights the heart of God when we all take our proper place in the human family, and affirm by our words and actions the intrinsic worth of each of its members.

I want to end with a story. It's rather an old story where I come from, but I'll keep my fingers crossed that you haven't all heard it. It's about a man who was tossing and turning one night because he couldn't get to sleep, when suddenly there stood at the end of his bed a figure who seemed to be glowing a bit in the dark, and who said: 'Don't be scared. I've come to grant you two wishes.' The man swallowed hard, thought for a bit and then said: 'I'd like to see heaven and I'd like to see hell'. 'That's a tall order' said the glowing one, who just might have been an angel, 'but I'll just give you a glimpse. Hell first.' And the man found himself looking at a scene of a great feast, with long, long tables groaning with food, and people sitting facing each other on both sides. And the food was even more delicious and mouth-watering, if such a thing is possible, than the food at Kanuga. But the people were looking quite miserable, for the one rule was that they were only allowed to eat by using a pole 6 feet long with a spike on the end, and try as they might, they couldn't get the food into their mouths. 'And now' said the glowing one, 'I'll show you heaven.' And the man found himself looking at exactly the same scene: the long table groaning with delicious food, the people sitting either side, the 6-foot poles with a spike on the end. The only difference was that now the people were feasting and talking and laughing together, for each one had taken the pole and was feeding his or her neighbour across the table.

29

A Different Kind of Kingdom

CHRIST THE KING SUNDAY 2004

Southwark Cathedral

There's a wonderful *rightness* for me in being in this place on this particular day, for I've known and loved this building for nearly fifty years. I've counted among my friends four of its Provosts and one of its Deans, from George Reindorp – still remembered in Salisbury (where I now live) as the bishop who was so sartorially aware that he even opted for purple Wellies – to Colin Slee, who doesn't share such grandiose tastes. In 1959, the eve of the consecration of Bishop Mervyn Stockwood, he spent the night in prayer in the Harvard Chapel, while I, as his chaplain, spent a marginally less uncomfortable night on a camp-bed in the vestry. Six years later, my wife and I were married by him where that altar now stands. Then, to our delight, our son Mark and his wife Joanie started worshipping here a couple of years ago, and found you to be a warm, welcoming and caring community; and today I'm here for the baptism, together with Theo, of our grand-daughter Ella Rachel. So it's all come together in a deeply satisfying way. And because it's come together on the feast day of Christ the King, I want very simply, in the context of this baptism and eucharist, to spell out what I believe this kingship to mean.

'Who do you say that I am?' Jesus once asked his disciples, for some were calling him a prophet, some Rabbi (meaning 'teacher'), and they usually called him 'Master'. But now, with a flash of insight, Peter says 'you – you are the Christ, the

Messiah'. By which he meant that Jesus was the one whom the Jews had long expected would be sent by God to deliver them from the occupying Romans and lead them to a glorious future. And, while Jesus doesn't deny that title, he tells them that he understands it in quite a different sense from that which Peter intended. Just as when, later, when Pilate asks Jesus 'Are you the King of the Jews' he replies: "King" is your word', implying that his understanding of kingship was utterly different from Pilate's. A few hours later Jesus was to die with the words 'This is Jesus, the king of the Jews' inscribed as a kind of cruel joke above his head. Though, amidst all the mockery, one of those crucified beside him had the insight to ask that Jesus would remember him when he came into his kingdom.

Now go back in your mind thirty years. John the Baptist is preaching in the wilderness, declaring that one is coming who will be so much greater than himself that he wasn't even worthy to stoop down and unfasten his sandals. Yet three years later, Jesus once again turns this worldly concept of greatness on its head when, supper being ended and within hours of his arrest, he takes a towel, kneels down, and does precisely that: unfastens his friends' sandals and washes their dusty feet. What all this suggests is that a true understanding of the God Jesus has come to reveal, and what our relationship with him and with each other is to mean, demands a complete reappraisal of how we view the true nature of power and authority. Faced with the life-changing truth about God that this Jesus whom they'd chosen to follow was revealing by his words and actions: that at the heart of creation is self-giving Love, they had to re-think the way they saw everything. They grasped that in God's terms greatness is defined in serving, not in being served; in loving because we are ourselves loved; in forgiving because we are forgiven. And when, very soon after his death and in the light of his resurrection, more and more people who wanted to follow Jesus came to be baptised into the infant church, St Paul tells

111

us that they chose as the first Christian creed the three words 'Jesus is Lord'. And they did so for two reasons: first, because 'Lord' was a name previously applied only to God and they had come to believe that Jesus was indeed the human face of God, that whatever else God may be in all his unimaginable majesty, all we need to know about him is that he is Christlike in his unchanging and affirming love. And second, they called him 'Lord' because the way of life he had taught was now to be authoritative in the lives of Christians. Paul's words in today's Epistle combine both truths: 'Christ is the image of the invisible God; his is the primacy over all creation'.

But they also called him 'King'. Christ the King. And they did so because the word he had used time and time again as he taught them about the ultimate purpose, the end for which the whole creation has been destined, that word was 'Kingdom': the Kingdom of God. A kingdom which isn't some far-off utopia, but one he had come to initiate. It's not a kingdom that Pilate would have understood, one dependent on the use of force, but rather an ordering of our common life based on Jesus' enduring values of love and forgiveness, justice and mercy, compassion and what Wordsworth called 'the little unremembered acts/Of kindness and of love'. What the Christian faith says is: 'Come and see, in the light of Jesus, what it means to be human in a world deeply divided between the haves and the have-nots, and a society whose less attractive marks are greed, aggression and contempt. Come and see what God looks like, and what every man, woman and child looks like to God, each one loved for what they uniquely are, so that you may learn to love them too. Come and see what creation looks like when you learn to see it as under the sovereignty of Christ.' I believe those first Christians understood what we so often forget when we become obsessed with the church and its tiresome altercations, that the church isn't an end in itself, but merely the principal agent, the instrument, for the building of something so much wider: the Kingdom. Thank God there have been some in every age who glimpsed that truth and who have sought, in however stumbling and inadequate a fashion, to live as people of his Kingdom, walking through the world as agents of his love.

Today Ella and Theo are to be baptised, and not simply made infant members of his church, but potential agents of the Kingdom. A Kingdom in which none is superior or inferior in worth, and the only privilege is serving others. A Kingdom in which each is valued not for what he or she *has* but for what he or she *is*: a unique child of God. A Kingdom in which we are called to see beyond the narrow loyalties of race or social class. For in the Kingdom the only solidarity that counts is that of our membership of the human race created in God's likeness. And, not least, a Kingdom whose keynotes are listening to those with whom we disagree, and in which we must forgive and, on our part, learn to receive forgiveness.

I end with some words from the first recorded teaching of Jesus in his home synagogue. Having read from Isaiah: 'The spirit of the Lord has sent me to announce good news to the poor, to proclaim release for prisoners ... and to let the broken victims go free', he begins to spell out their implications in terms of love and justice. And they were offended and drove him from their midst. And when he persisted in challenging their legalism with the radical new standards of God's Kingdom, they finally allowed him his title of 'King', but nailed it and him to a cross. 'He claims to be our king,' they mocked; 'so let him reign from there!'

The existence of this cathedral, and the existence of every other church in Christendom, and the bringing of Ella and Theo to be baptised in the name of Christ the King, witness to the fact that he does.

Part Two

On Various Occasions

30

Installation as Dean of Westminster

7 JULY 1986

Westminster Abbey

First things first. I pay tribute to my old friend and teacher, Bishop Edward Knapp-Fisher, who during a lengthy inter-regnum has served the Abbey as its Sub-Dean with meticulous and loving care, so that the Abbey family is greatly in his debt. His energy is astonishing, only matched by that of my much-loved, cycling predecessor. Thirty years ago Edward Knapp-Fisher was Principal of the College where I learned to be a priest, and the summons we most feared was a firm hand on the shoulder after lunch and the words 'Care for a walk?': not so much an invitation as a command. It was known as 'the Grind' and covered much of the county of Oxfordshire. Last month, on a brief holiday in Austria, Bishop Edward was still walking twenty miles a day. We thank God for his health and for his wise counsel and judgment during these past months.

I should explain to the Queen's scholars of Westminster School, as perhaps the first Chairman of Governors to have failed his 'O' level Latin, that that was the Cambridge pronunciation. When I learned of the Latin oath, I remembered a close friend of mine, equally bereft of a classical education, who went to a weekday Eucharist at an old-fashioned Anglo-Catholic church for the first time and found himself the only member of the congregation. At the Offertory the priest turned to him and said 'Dominus vobiscum'. For a moment he panicked, his mind desperately searching for an answer, only to come up with the inspired reply: 'Et tu, Brute'.

In a recent book the Roman Catholic writer, Fr. Gerard Hughes, suggests that it can be a useful exercise to write your own obituary notice, not the obituary you fear you might get, but the kind you would love to have. He suggests that this is the way to discover those desires which are at the core of your inner life, and which motivate you.

Now it may be both rash and foolish, for one who has been its Dean for a mere fifteen minutes, to suggest, as it were, an obituary for this Abbey, but I want to try to set out the frame-work of the obituary I would desire for it; and I hope such an exercise may both reflect what I have already sensed about this place, its values and its tradition, and also convey some of my own priorities.

I would want a perceptive obituarist to spot certain facets of the life of this place which speak of its nature, its purpose and its goal. And the first would be that at the end of the 20th century the spirit of the medieval Benedictine community, in terms of its common life in Christ, its warmth and its hospitality, had been maintained. I see as a prime charge upon me the building up of the body of Christ in love, in the spirit of those marvellous words I have just read from the letter to the Philippians, and I count myself lucky that my two immediate predecessors shared that vision and have done so much to help create an Abbey family which is not just a pious hope but a tangible reality.

Secondly, I would want our obituarist to record that we cared about quality: that, whether in the planning of worship or the administration of our affairs we were meticulous. Not perfectionist in a fussy, obsessive sense, but in that rigorous giving attention to detail which is all of a piece with the giving attention to people which we call love, and the giving attention to God which we call worship.

How tempting and easy it must be for a cathedral or abbey to switch the controls to 'automatic', and for its worship or the ministry it provides to people to begin to lose something of their quality or their style. However different the scale, we must give the same quality of thought and attention to a memorial service on a wet Monday in November, or to a daily Evensong, as we give to a Royal Wedding. Many, many people come here just once, and how they are received and what they see and hear may help them to a deeper understanding of the beauty and the love of God.

Third: for long years, my obituarist will note, the Abbey was encased in scaffolding. I hope he will not draw the same conclusion as Jan Morris, writing of Wells Cathedral in *The Times*: 'It crossed my mind, indeed, so ubiquitous were the symptoms of restoration, that the Cathedral's chief function had become its own repairs'.

On the contrary, our likely decade under scaffolding, and the restoration already achieved, is a sign that we take very seriously both our debt to the past and our need to keep faith with future generations in caring for this incomparable place. The good stewardship of our fabric only becomes dangerously self-absorbed where it is not matched by a generous – and the Gospels would suggest a reckless – giving to the needs of the poor and the deprived. I shall be concerned to see that the Benedictine tradition of loving and generous hospitality continues to extend to neighbours in the inner cities of our own land, as well as those in the Third World; which is why the retiring collection today will go to a scheme for disadvantaged and unemployed young people in the North East.

The fourth fact about the Abbey which a future obituarist could not fail to see is that it is a meeting place of the nations. A press photographer asked me last week: 'Do they have any services in there or is it just for tourists?' Tourists – or pilgrims? And where do you draw the dividing line, or analyse the motives of the three to four million people of widely divergent cultures who now visit the Abbey every year. That they have the right to come to this historic place is not in doubt, and it is not for a new Dean to raise at this time the

119

vexed question of how you best demonstrate that we are not a museum or a mausoleum but a living community and a place whose chief task is the worship and praise of God.

What concerns me more is the role the Abbey must play for the people those pilgrim/tourists represent: those on the fringe of the Christian life – or quite outside it – who come consciously or unconsciously seeking God. Perhaps on a Sunday because in a large church you can be anonymous; perhaps to a lunchtime service on a weekday; perhaps to one of our innumerable special services. And perhaps many come because they know instinctively that an abbey such as this stands for stability, for permanent and humane values at a time of great change and uncertainty.

The Dean of St Paul's has written of the huge number of seekers of the faith who now come to our cathedrals or their equivalent. He writes that we have the task of preaching the Gospel in such a way as to communicate with the person who is half-interested, and suggests that only on radio or television do similar opportunities exist for 'speaking across the frontier which normally divides the ordinary workaday world from the ecclesiastical'.

I believe our task here is to preach and teach a Gospel which speaks clearly, intelligently, and in terms people can understand, of the powerful mysteries of our faith: of the unique, irreplaceable nature of each one of us; of the fact that God is in love with us and of that love and forgiveness as it is disclosed in Jesus Christ; of how we may recognise the signs of the Kingdom of God; of the new life in the Spirit experienced by those whose lives are centred on the breaking and sharing of bread in the Eucharist.

In the best sense, I would have our obituarist say, the Abbey was a *teaching* church, because its preachers listened to, and sought to answer, the questions people actually asked. But that in no way conflicted with the fact that it was a *questioning* church, aware that a church which is a pilgrim church, if it is not to be bland or complacent, will always be open and questioning, continually developing in its understanding of the mysteries of God.

The Abbey holds a special place in the affections of the world-wide Anglican Communion, and it is the distinctive mark and strength of Anglicanism that, while it is a deeply scriptural faith, which places equal emphasis on Word and Sacraments, it is tolerant and comprehensive and allows its members a great freedom of theological exploration.

A teaching church and a questioning church will include within its walls many whose faith is very fragile; and that implies a third quality, that of *listening*. We need to listen to the questions people are asking, yes, and hear the pain and quiet desperation in many lives. We also need to listen to those who differ from us. All our insights into truth are partial ones, and the truth, as Charles Simeon of Cambridge said a hundred and fifty years ago, 'may often lie not between two extremes, but in both extremes.' Nothing is so destructive as the doctrinaire certainties of those divided by political or theological conviction, whether in Parliament or the General Synod, who simply cannot or will not listen to what those opposed to them are actually saying, nor bother to discover why they think as they do. I hope the Abbey's concern with ecumenical and inter-faith dialogue and activities will continue, based as it is on the belief that it is the one God in whom each one of us 'lives and moves and has his being'. It was Macaulay who said that the Abbey is 'a great temple of reconciliation ...'.

'A great temple of reconciliation' and he added: 'and silence'. And by 'silence' I take him to mean a place concerned with the practice of the presence of God. Whatever my imaginary obituarist may write, we shall have failed in our purpose and our goal if he does not judge that what we are chiefly about, always have been about and always will be about, is the worship of God. Unless this is a house of prayer it is nothing. Nothing we do is as important as the daily and

121

weekly round of Office and Eucharist and waiting upon God: worshipping him with the sense of awe appropriate in the presence of sheer goodness. Nothing matters more than that rare experience of being caught up out of yourself in wonder, perhaps at the beauty of the music, or by that momentary sense that you are in a fearful and holy place where for nearly a thousand years men and women have sought and found the presence of God. As the writer of this month's Abbey prayer leaflet rightly says: 'The questions a new Dean has constantly to ask of himself and of others are: "Is this service designed to help people worship God?" and "Is this a house of prayer?" '

I want to end on a rather more personal note to members of the Abbey family. The last time I stood in this pulpit was to preach at the Consecration of John Austin Baker. I ended by pleading with John to learn to say 'no'; to carve out of his diary a space so that he could continue to speak to people of God by that inner stillness which is born of silence and prayer and proper time for recreation and relaxation. I will try to take my own advice. And also I shall try not to take either myself or my office with a solemnity neither deserve. If I had been told thirty years ago that I would one day be Dean of Westminster I should have laughed at the absurdity of it. A bit of me still does and, please God, will continue to do so.

'I just want a normal life' sings Adelaide in *Guys and Dolls*, 'with wallpaper and bookends'. Well, so do I; and instead look what I've got. This amazing Abbey, and twenty-six ex-Deans on my landing. And a heap of expectations. I remember Cardinal Hume saying when he was made Archbishop of Westminster (and what a joy to have him here today): 'There is a frightening gap between what is expected of me and what I know myself to be. But I take comfort from the fact that it's quite healthy to feel small and inadequate, and to know that anything you are going to achieve will depend on God.' And I want to say to you right at the start: I am not Elijah, nor one of the prophets, nor am I Eric Abbot, or Edward Carpenter. I am me. And you must let me be myself and in my own way try to minister to you, listen to you and love you, as together we seek to be open to what the Spirit is saying to us in the years ahead. All I know is that whatever it may be the Abbey is called to do and be during my time as its Dean, certain things do not change: we are called first and foremost to worship and trust God, to centre our lives on Christ, and to be open to his Spirit. And to echo the simple words of Dag Hammarskjöld:

> For all that has been – Thanks!
> To all that shall be – Yes!

31

Tolerance

25 SEPTEMBER 1988

Washington National Cathedral

A fortnight ago, sitting in my study whose windows open into Westminster Abbey, with the sound of a thousand American tourists buzzing about like bees, I asked myself: what do I most want to say in Washington Cathedral? And I thought I should like to speak of what bothers me most about the Church in Britain. A parting of the ways with the coming of women priests? No; something more subtle and potentially more damaging. The growth of a divisive, reactionary and intolerant spirit: the fact that it is often not the enemies of the Faith who scare me, but its friends, not those who are against us but those on our side.

And so I turned to the Gospel for today. At first sight it seemed unhelpful. 'Anyone who is not against us' said Jesus, when his disciples protest that some maverick healer is using his name, 'anyone who is not against us is for us.' Then I turned to the Epistle. That didn't seem much better. 'Who are you' writes James, 'to give a verdict on your neighbour?' Who am I indeed? Who am I to be critical in public or in private about those whose understanding of God and whose understanding of the Gospel is different from mine?

And yet my fear persists and will be heard. For it is precisely this point of the wrongness, the danger of the passing of judgment which lies at the heart of my concern. And it should always be possible to speak the truth as we see it in love. Let me explain.

Jesus often spoke of people being hungry and thirsty for God. Not religious people: just people; and many today are wanting to explore the things of the spirit. This isn't surprising for each person is made in the likeness of God and there is within us all a kind of homesickness; and we are strangely moved when, for example, we hear St Augustine's words about the heart being restless until it find rest in God.

But human beings are mysterious and complex creatures. Any one of us may appear strong and confident, yet we are most of us fragile and vulnerable and unconfident people, needing to love and be loved, yet often hurt or damaged, and needing to be consoled before we can believe. And the truths of the Gospel, these great mysteries of God's grace which have to do with the deepest questions of human existence, these the Church must handle with care and proclaim with an eloquent but profound humility.

What I find a little scary is the look in the eyes of those who preach an exclusive and intolerant kind of Gospel, with its emphasis on sin and judgment, with its total unwavering certainty, which can only conceive of conversion in black-and-white, born-again terms, and does not see human beings as the complex creatures we are, whose journey towards God – a journey of mind as well as heart – is not often so simply achieved.

One of the lovely gifts of the Spirit – historically, a very Anglican gift – is that of tolerance. And it is the idea of tolerance that informs both St James in the Epistle when he tells us to avoid passing judgment on each other, and of Jesus in the Gospel when he apparently refuses to condemn any who claim to speak in his name, and asserts that anyone – believer or unbeliever – who gives a cup of water to one who is thirsty is blessed by God for that action alone.

To be tolerant doesn't mean to be weak or indecisive, nor that you regard all opinions equally valid. It means that you understand that human motives and human behaviour are complex, and that you yourself are often blind to the truth; it means that you believe, with St John, that God enlightens the mind of every person who comes into the world and therefore that you pay attention to, and take with seriousness, all on the human journey; it means that our Church has often been prepared to tolerate for the time being what may appear to be error; it means that you know that God alone is true, and that no one person or party or church has a monopoly of truth.

It is so easy to divide people into sheep and goats, those who have seen the light and those who are in the dark – and already in the New Testament you can see signs of the early Church seeking to do just that by the emphases it places on certain sayings of Jesus as it compiles its Gospels; but we have neither the right nor the ability to do so. And the Church is always unattractive when it becomes exclusive rather than inclusive; when it appears unsympathetic to those who in their own way are seeking the truth, or judgmental of those who are unable or unwilling to make their own the credal and moral packages on offer. Yet such people are often drawn to God by strange compulsions, for ever surprising a hunger in themselves.

But which more truly would seem to express the way of Christ: to say to such pilgrims: 'Believe this and you are in the fold and may claim Church membership', or to say: 'Come and sit where we sit, and hear what we hear and see what we see. Come and experience the reality of worship and then, perhaps, little by little, the truth of the love of God as that is seen in the life and teaching and Passion and Resurrection of Jesus Christ will find a place in your heart'?

If a narrow exclusivity is an offence against the mystery of the human spirit, there can also be the handing out of what I would call 'packaged religion' which is an offence against the mystery of the Gospel. A readiness happily to swallow down the great mysteries of the Catholic faith undigested – all neatly labelled: the Virgin Birth, the Atonement, the Resurrection, the Trinity – and to swallow them down, as someone has said, 'like a plump cat devouring large morsels of food with a licking of lips and a smug wiping of whiskers, as if the fact that these morsels are hard to swallow makes this prompt dispatch (with scarcely a gulp or a hiccup) something virtuous and creditable.'

Don't misunderstand. There is a sense in which the truths we are to live by: the truth of the Fatherhood of God and his love for us, the story of the Passion of Christ and his rising again, are truths that a child can grasp, and indeed the Kingdom of God can only be entered by those with a child-like spirit of openness and trust. But the mystery of God made man, the mystery of our redemption, of love crucified, of the glory of Christ's suffering, of the nature of Resurrection life: these are inexhaustible mysteries. And the true religious quest, it has been said, is a series of revelations, but the revelations are of one luminous mystery after another. Being a Christian may often mean speaking into the dark in hope and trust, and an over-assertive and over-simplistic proclaiming of the faith may mask an intolerant and judgmental spirit which effectively turns away those who would know God and look to the Church to help them.

'Who will give us meat to eat?' demand the people of Moses in the Old Testament reading we heard today. And so I come back to my starting point. Many are hungry for God and for the one who is the living bread. But they fear the image of God as he is often portrayed: stern and judgmental, demanding obedience and watchful for every fault.

I believe Martin Luther spoke truly when he said that 'Christ's proper work is to declare the grace of God, to console and to enliven'. For Jesus comes to call sinners, but he invites, he does not condemn. And always, *always*, he addresses a particular person where he or she is, in his or her need. When he declares the grace of God he does it within a particular encounter. When he consoles he is consoling this man or that woman, Levi, Zaccheus, Bartimaus, Mary Magdalene, the woman at the well, the woman taken in adultery, the woman with the issue of blood, the young man led down by his friends through the roof. He declares the grace of God, he consoles and he *enlivens*, in the sense that new life arises from each encounter. And those who watch him, in all his liberating compassion, are amazed and, sometimes, scandalized.

But what is the real scandal is that ever since some have used the Gospel of God's wrath and not his love; a Gospel of impending judgment to bring people to their knees in fear and trembling.

Do we not yet understand? It is, says St Paul, the nature of love to make excuse for every fault in the beloved. Do we not yet understand, as Luther did, that we need to be consoled before we can repent? We need to know ourselves loved by the God whose love is unconditional, and who makes excuses for our every fault.

Our Strange and Marvellous
Human Diversity

29 SEPTEMBER 1991

St Paul's Church, Waco, Texas

A flurry of letters and faxes passed between your Rector and me. 'What would you like me to preach about?' I asked. In reply, he sent the lessons set for this morning. I then sent him a fax: 'They're a bit grim' I said, 'but I'll have a shot.' 'I agree', he faxed back. 'Feel free to preach about anything you wish.'

Now *that's* how to make your guests feel at home. And I do, at once, and not just because of your Rector's thoughtfulness. Let me explain.

Every Sunday my colleagues and I stand in the nave of Westminster Abbey saying goodbye to the hundreds of visitors after the Abbey Eucharist. They come from Spain and Italy, Sweden and Japan, Nigeria and South India – but chiefly, it must be said, from the United States: from Boston and Pittsburgh, Charleston and Sheboygan, and (when we are especially lucky) from Waco. And they come from many different traditions, everything from Southern Baptist to Roman Catholic. It's a bit like the day of Pentecost when people from a score of different nations were caught up in an experience of worshipping God which overcame and transcended all their differences of language and culture. It's a weekly reminder of St Paul's claim that 'we were all baptized into one body in a single Spirit'.

But within the extreme diversity of this worldwide Christian family there are those whose history and life-style have brought them together into a particular tradition within the whole. And the fact that I can leave my Westminster Abbey Eucharist and drop out of the sky into your Eucharist here in the heart of Texas, and feel completely at home, is not just because of our common baptism into Christ and our common belief in God. It also has to do with our membership of this remarkable body, born out of the turmoil of the Reformation, that we call the Anglican Church.

You may not think of yourselves first and foremost as Episcopalians any more than I think of myself as first and foremost a member of the Church of England. For we're not. First and foremost we are Christians, sharing a common faith in the God revealed in Jesus Christ. But we can't deny our history, and until that great day when the church is visibly united in all its God-given diversity, we must witness to those particular insights of our own tradition. We must witness to *our* way of doing things, to a spirit which is distinctive and different and therefore important. Why? Because the truth of the mystery of God is greater than we can know, and we must each witness to the truth in our way and as we see it.

'Anyone who is not against us is for us' said Jesus in today's Gospel which tells of how his disciples protest when some maverick healer uses Christ's name; and 'who are you to give a verdict on your neighbour?' writes St James sharply in today's Epistle. Both remarks suggest that it's unwise ever to be judgmental or intolerant about others who in their own fashion are seeking the truth about God or the mystery of our existence.

And it is precisely the judgmental nature of those who, on both sides of the Atlantic, seem to me to be preaching an exclusive and intolerant kind of Christianity that most needs to be challenged. And it is challenged by that element in the Anglican tradition that is its most striking feature even though Anglicans don't have a monopoly on it: a spirit of tolerance or forbearance.

Those who need an authoritarian church, those who look for a neatly labelled package of belief delivered from on high that cannot be questioned, are simply not true to the spirit of that Anglicanism that was hammered out in the 16th and 17th centuries and that has taken root and flourished in a wealth of different nations and cultures. I mean the belief that no one person, or party or church, has a monopoly of the truth. The belief that the truth rarely lies in this or that extreme view, but may indeed lie in both extremes. That's why our Anglican Church has been slow to condemn extreme opinions, but has always fought to hold together within one body people of the most diverse views. And this comprehensiveness, this ability to celebrate diversity, to celebrate the strengths of the Anglo-Catholic, the conservative evangelical, the liberal and charismatic, the searcher and the doubter, within the one fellowship and family is often uncomfortable. But, it is both realistic in terms of our human nature; and it is faithful to the God revealed in the Gospel of Christ.

To value forbearance, to value tolerance, is to recognize two deep truths: the first about us human beings, and the second about the God in whose image we are made.

It is to recognize the human truth that for each of us the way to the God who is both our journey and our journey's end will be different, dictated by our personality and our experience of life. Within every congregation there will be some whom life has treated gently and some whom life has knocked flat time and time again; some who are sociable, others who are shy and self-contained; some who know themselves loved, others who can't accept they have any value even to God; some who are thankful, others who are hurt or angry or confused. People, in other words, just like you and me – for at times don't we feel all those things in ourselves? Isn't this what it means to be human, and doesn't this colour our experience of God and our ability to respond to the truth as that is revealed in Christ?

131

The second truth which is safeguarded by what I have called our Anglican spirit of forbearance is that the God revealed in Jesus is a tolerant and forbearing God. The simple over-arching truth which unites all Christians is the belief that God became incarnate in Jesus Christ, and in this man invites our response. The God who is Love knows no other way: he leaves us free. Free to reject him, free to respond to him. Free to crown him in our hearts as King: free to crown him with thorns. The Christ comes, in Martin Luther's words, 'to declare the grace of God, to console and to enliven', and the Gospel shows Jesus inviting individuals, in encounter after encounter, to respond to this God, this awesome yet gentle and tolerant God, who loves them more than they can conceive, and who is indeed both their journey and their journey's end.

Sunday by Sunday, for me at Westminster Abbey, for you here at St Paul's, our lives centre on an encounter with the God we have begun to come to know in Jesus Christ in the weekly breaking and sharing of bread at the Eucharist. Our congregation and yours are just two tiny cells in the world-wide body of those who are seeking to give attention to the mystery. The mystery of the God who, having declared himself in Jesus, now invites our response. The God who knows our failure and our need. He invites us to his feast, not as we should like to be and one day may be, but (thank God) as we *are* in all our strange and marvellous human diversity.

33

For My Father

17 NOVEMBER 1991

St Andrew Church, Harlestone

'The Lord shall rehearse it when he writeth up the people: that he was born there.' Psalm 87:6.

For most of you this is a very ordinary occasion, the only difference being that, in place of your American Rector preaching, or your local Lay Reader, you have a preacher from London. For me, it is a quite extraordinary one.

For I was born here. Born in the old Rectory just over sixty years ago and baptized in that font. My father, also Michael, was Rector from 1928–33, and this was his pulpit. I have a photograph album full of me in the pram in the Rectory garden, me taking my first staggering steps on the Rectory terrace, me on my first tricycle circumnavigating the rose beds. And then, one day in May 1933, the photographs come to an end. For on that day my father climbed the tower of this church and threw himself from the top. He was killed almost instantaneously.

Such were the harsh rulings of the day that a suicide was not allowed Christian burial so he has no marked grave in the churchyard. Instead his ashes were scattered to the winds.

You will therefore understand why this is for me a strangely disconcerting sort of day, one of those when life seems to come full circle. And you will I hope forgive me if I speak much more personally than I normally would.

I can't really remember my father. A few of you still living in the the village will remember him, as does Elsie Gerald, who has come all the way from Brighton to share this day with me. And I believe Earl Spencer, as a very small boy, was present at my Baptism. They tell me my father was popular in the village, human, well-liked, charming, with a good sense of humour. His death, then, must have been all the more shocking. I shall never know for sure the reasons for it. I am told he left a note, which my mother later understandably destroyed. (She, incidentally, is still alive, a very active and independent 90-year-old living in Devon.)

I feel for my father both compassion and gratitude. Compassion because suicide is an act of desperation arising out of deep unhappiness which in his case he seems, as a very private person, to have kept to himself. And gratitude because he gave me the supreme gift of life.

But you may ask: why come back to a place where such a tragedy occurred? Isn't all that so far in the past as to be forgotten, irrelevant and of no possible interest to the people of Harlestone? So let me attempt to answer that question. I have come back to Harlestone this morning for four reasons.

First and most simply, because, although it's been a pretty nomadic life ever since, I was born here. This in a very real sense is home. For it was in the protection of that house and garden, in the beauty of this village with its ironstone houses, these lanes and this parkland, that I first grew aware of and responded to the beauty of the world.

Secondly, I have come back because I want to say that it is only at a surface level that life is merely a chronology of events. Certain happenings are so traumatic and go so deep that they are like an earthquake, quite changing the pattern of what ensues. Most of you will have known in the past the devastating effect of an accident, a death, the breakdown of a marriage, which not only touches you at a deep level but actually changes the whole pattern of your life. The loss of a father or a mother in infancy is with you for life.

Thirdly, I have come back in order to say: what matters is not so much what happens to us and our loved ones in this unpredictable world, but how we respond, what we make of what we receive. What matters is whether we believe that there is no experience which cannot be redeemed. That is the central meaning of the Cross of Christ: that good may be brought out of evil. That out of something as destructively and apparently final new life arose. And I have come back to say – and I simply don't know if this will make sense to you – but I have come back to say to my father who is now alive in God, and in this place that he loved and served: 'It's all right. The potential damage of your sudden death was contained. We survived. And, by the grace of God, we did more than survive, for we brought something creative out of what seemed only destructive, something joyful (I speak here of my mother's full and largely happy life, my own good marriage and family and my priesthood), something good out of what was so desperate a cry for help and so devastating an event for those who loved you.'

Now don't misunderstand me. We can stand and plead for one another before the throne of God but we cannot undo the free action of another or stand in their place. We are each our own unique selves and answer for our own unique actions. And I'm not a priest in order in some way to atone for my father's destructive act, nor (so far as I know) did his death have anything to do with my response to God's call when it came. But I *am* flesh of his flesh, and bone of his bone, and there is in truth that of my father in me which helps to make me what I am, and which makes it (to say the least) feel good and right to be standing once again where he so often stood.

I have come because I was born here. I have come because what happened all that time ago deeply changed my life. I have come because I believe that there is nothing which cannot be redeemed and because I want to say to my father: 'It's all right.' But there is a fourth and final reason why it's good to be here. If I have learned anything in my ministry –

135

and perhaps the fact of my father's suicide helped me to learn it – it is that none of us dare pass judgment on the life of another. That is God's prerogative, and his judgment is always more than matched by his mercy. Those who become embittered by what life has done to them, or those who feel so trapped or so despairing that they take their own life, may have had the dice loaded against them from the start, and none of us know whether we should survive if we had been in their place.

What we do know is that the God who is our judge is also our saviour, and that in Jesus Christ all we need to know of God is once and for all defined. He has made him known in the only terms we can understand: in human terms. His every word and action is radiated by his knowledge of his heavenly Father, and so we can now say that God is like a man who heals the sick and loves the sinner; who takes a basin and towel and washes his disciples' feet; who, when nailed to a cross, forgives those who are nailing him there. Jesus knows the Father to be wholly Love, and that to be reconciled to God is to be caught up into 'a love that will not let us go', a love beyond our present imagining.

Jesus sought out and consoled the despairing; he welcomed sinners; he described God as a Father waiting and watching for his penitent child; he hung on a cross out of love for us. The God Jesus Christ reveals is not merely our Creator who knows our inmost hearts but also our Redeemer who, even as we turn to him in penitence, has forgiven us and welcomed us home.

I do not believe my father needs me to tell him that. I believe that when he fell from this tower he was in a deeper sense caught and held in the everlasting arms of the one who is the merciful Father of us all. But I believe I needed after all these years to express these truths in this place – and I am grateful to you for allowing me to do so.

34

Courage, Love, and Hope

19 NOVEMBER 1991

Westminster Abbey

I welcome you to the Abbey at this time of great thanks-giving. Not many months before he was taken hostage Terry Waite preached from that pulpit, and every day since he was taken hostage we, like so many thousands of other churches, have remembered him by name at one of our services. Now we come to express our gratitude to God for the safe return home of Terry Waite and Tom Sutherland, and to pray for the release of those still held hostage and for the peace of our world.

This is not an occasion for many words. Yet there are three words whose meaning for me has been illuminated by what Terry Waite is and by what he has achieved.

The first word is *courage*: courage both physical and moral. You will remember why Terry Waite went to Beirut. It was on a humanitarian mission to plead for the release of others held hostage. His friends strongly advised him not to go back into the complex, violent world of Lebanon. He might, they said, be risking his life. He listened to this advice and – foolishly no doubt as the world judges these things – he ignored it. He believed he had no choice. It was for him both a matter of conscience and of Christian discipleship. And indeed it is consistent with the life of a man who seeks to follow the one who chose to go up to Jerusalem even when it meant almost certain crucifixion. Terry's return to Lebanon showed the kind of foolhardy courage which may well be demanded of those who at their baptism are marked with a cross.

If my first word is courage, my second is *love*. It is when we display a certain quality of love that we are most God-like, most Christ-like. The love of which I speak is not an emotion, a feeling, but the costly, deliberate, chosen giving of yourself – even, if it comes to it, your life – for the sake of another. And it has cost Terry five lost years of the kind of privation and suffering few of us can begin to imagine.

Courage. Love. My third word is *hope*. I said my three words were illuminated not just by what Terry Waite *is* but by what he has *achieved*. Can a man shackled to a wall for nearly five years achieve anything? Yes, a great deal; for what he has done is to demonstrate to a world so often dragged down by our human capacity for evil the true quality and strength of the human spirit under extreme pressure. Terry would be the first to remind us that the other hostages, and the spirit with which they have emerged from captivity, have an equal claim to our admiration and gratitude. Good is seen to be ultimately more powerful than evil; love more effective than hate. A hostage's spirit of endurance, that unembittered and quiet strength that was so evident three months ago in John McCarthy and last night and today in Terry Waite, these give us renewed hope in the humanity we all share.

That Terry Waite has come home is a cause for great rejoicing: a kind of resurrection after a very long and dark time. We thank God for him; we thank God with his family and friends; and we thank God that the candles that have burned in so many places for Terry have been the symbol of lasting and eternal truths.

35

The Absurd Generosity of Grace

19 SEPTEMBER 1993

St Paul's Church, Waco, Texas

Alison and I are enormously indebted to you for giving us the chance of coming back to Waco and to St Paul's, for the warmth of your friendship two years ago gave us one of our happiest memories of the States; and we were not going to let slip the chance of coming again.

However, sitting this week for eleven long, uncomfortable hours on an American Airlines jet in what is called 'thrift class', drinking large amounts of Sprite to prevent dehydration, eating plastic food from plastic containers, I could not help thinking how frustrating it was that those who have been rather more successful in worldly terms were reclining in club class and quite probably drinking champagne. An airliner is an unusually contained example of the have-mores and the have-lesses, all travelling hopefully but not all being treated alike.

In this world, on the whole, you get what you pay for. But today's Gospel suggests that rather different principles apply when it comes to God's Kingdom. The stories Jesus tells almost always ask of us a total shift in what we consider to be of value. The world may understand greatness and success in terms of prestige and rewards – club class or thrift – and of exercising control over others; but Jesus says that in the Kingdom of God greatness is judged in terms of the costly, time-consuming giving of yourself to others, like – well, like kneeling to wash their dusty feet.

The world may understand life in terms of *doing*, competing, achieving, judging; Jesus sees it in terms of *being*, listening, rejoicing in other's gifts, sharing in their sorrows.

The world may speak of revenge and retribution, 'an eye for an eye, a tooth for a tooth'; Jesus speaks of forgiveness without measure. His aim, always, is to point to the Kingdom; his message never less than life-changing. For the Kingdom describes the condition of those whose eyes have been opened to the true nature of God, and who succeed here and there and now and then in acting and living in a Christlike way. In the Kingdom the only power is that of love, the only criterion that of justice, the only true freedom that of those who acknowledge the Kingship of Christ. And Christ establishes the Church as the agent that exists to bring the Kingdom into being, to give us glimpses of what a true community under God could be like.

And it is just because we find it so hard to picture the Kingdom that Jesus nudges us towards it in story after story and says: Look! It's like this. It's like that. It's like the wonder of finding a treasure or a pearl hidden in a field; it's like the joy of finding something you had lost and thought you would never find again; for God, it's like the joy a parent feels when their child comes home again after many years' absence. It's like a great banquet where all are treated the same and rich and poor sit side by side.

Or, as we've just heard, it's like workmen in a vineyard hired at different times of the day who in the evening each get paid the same. If in this world, by and large, you get what you pay for and you earn what you deserve, in the Kingdom you don't. You all get the same and it has nothing to do with what you earn or what you deserve. The last to be hired is paid just as much as the one who has worked all day. Why?

In a very similar story to be found three hundred years later in the Jewish Talmud the employer explains that it's quite fair for the last to be paid the same as the first because they have worked twice as hard. But that's not what Jesus says. He says that when they complain about unjust treatment the employer replies: 'But it's quite fair. You agreed with me to accept the standard wage. Take what I promised you. I happen to want to give this last man the same as I gave you. Are you jealous because I am generous?'

See that as a story about industrial relations and it's a recipe for disaster. See it as a story about the nature of God and rewards in his Kingdom and there could not be a more striking illustration of the sheer, unearned grace of God who chooses in his generosity to value each of us alike and offers us in Christ his unstinted love. God is the employer; and our reward at the end of the day is a new quality of life in Christ which not even death can take away.

As with many of the parables of Jesus, this story has a general and eternal truth, and a more specific historical application. The eternal truth, the one that matters, is that God loves each of us equally: all are called and all shall have prizes. So God in his love says in Christ: 'Are you jealous because I love each of you alike?'

The historical setting in the Gospels is undoubtedly Jesus' controversy with the Pharisees who are deeply shocked that he admits to his company tax collectors, social outcasts and obvious sinners, eats with them and invites them to open their eyes and glimpse the Kingdom. Over and over again Jesus says to good and decent and religious people – and we'd better hear this truth because no doubt today we are among them – that if they think they can secure a special place in God's love by their prayers, their church-going or their behaviour, then they may have had the experience but they've missed the meaning – just as one of your children would be wrong if he or she thought that by being good, by conforming, you would love him or her more than you do. You love each for their own unique selves with a love that is not dependent on their behaviour.

So the complaining workman who says 'it's unfair. I've borne the burden and the heat of day' is kin to the joyless

141

elder brother in the story of the Prodigal Son. 'What about me, then? It's so unfair. All this singing and dancing and fatted calves being killed and you and our mother beside yourselves with joy because my wastrel of a brother has come home. I've worked for you for years and never disobeyed you. I don't get roast kid and the red carpet laid out.' And his father says: 'Son, you are always with me, all I have is yours.'

In other words, God, in the absurd generosity of his love, loves both alike; and in Christ invites us to live as those who, while still part of the divided, unjust world, accept that in the Kingdom each of us is loved and valued for the unique and irreplaceable person we are.

Which is exactly the point made in the central activity of our common life in Christ: this eucharistic meal which week by week gives a tiny foretaste of the Kingdom of God. Whoever we are, rich or poor, black or white, life-long Christians or those newly admitted to the faith, we kneel at his table and receive our share of the living bread. We each receive the same. And the gift could not be greater. And we have done nothing to deserve or earn it.

Once we see that, the story of the labourers in the vineyard makes perfect sense. In the Kingdom there is no place for envy or jealousy or spiritual pride. What God offers each of us is a relationship of love that will be totally fulfilling. He asks of us only that we gratefully, like a child receiving a gift, trust him and hold out our open hands.

36

My Father

MAY 1996

St Paul's Cathedral

I hope you will understand if I speak today in unusually personal terms; and when I have done so, I think you will know why today is so special for me – and much more than just another preaching engagement in my second favourite church in London.

I am an only child and my father was a priest, the rector of a small, idyllic country parish in Northamptonshire. He was older than my mother whom he had married when he moved to his parish in 1928, and in the following year I was born. I still have the old photograph albums and all my earliest memories are of that delectable time: me in my pram in the huge rectory garden; me taking my first halting steps clutching a stuffed rabbit; me on my first tricycle circumnavigating the rose-beds. My mother appears in scores of them: my father perhaps half-a-dozen times. And then, after a brief four years, the photographs come to an end. For on a Saturday afternoon in May, while my mother was out shopping, my father wrote a brief note to her, climbed the tower of his church beside the rectory, removed the boarding from the belfry and threw himself down. The gardener found him but he died almost at once.

My mother was left homeless, with £40 in the world. She turned for help either to the Clergy Orphan Corporation or to the Sons of the Clergy; I cannot now discover which. But it doesn't much matter, for in your archives there will be thousands of similar cases of need.

In those harsh days a suicide was allowed no proper burial, no marked grave or memorial. 'I cannot conceive of a clergyman' said the coroner at the inquest, 'desecrating holy ground, as Mr Mayne has done, unless his mind was very much deranged.' My father's ashes were scattered to the four winds, and no-one ever spoke of him again. When I was fifteen I was told the brief facts by my mother, but nothing more; what he was like, this unhappy man whose genes I carry, or what deep unhappiness led him to take such a desperate action, I could only guess. In the words of a friend of mine (Frederick Buechner) who was ten when his own father took his life: 'The sadness is that you have lost a father you have never fully found. It's like a tune that ends before you have heard it out. Your whole life through you search to catch the strain, and seek the face you have lost in strangers' faces.'

So that was that – until last year. For sometimes life comes full circle in the strangest, least predictable of ways, and there is a kind of healing.

Eighteen months ago, and after a lifetime's silence, a letter arrived from the present rector saying that a few people in my father's village still remember what for them in their teenage years was a traumatic event, and that they would like to see a simple memorial stone placed in his old church. I was moved by the offer and asked a good friend, a fine Irish sculptor, Ken Thompson, to carve a stone with my father's name and dates.

And then, one hot Sunday last August, on my mother's 94th birthday, we brought her back to the village with her grandchildren and great-grandchildren, and at the morning Eucharist the stone was dedicated by the suffragan bishop and I stood in my father's pulpit sixty years on and tried to find the right words with which to tell the father I had never really known – what? That I forgave him? That all was well? Yes, that certainly, but other things too.

I knew, as I stood in his pulpit, that I was not in some way claiming to atone by my own priesthood for my father's destructive act. We are each our own unique and responsible selves and answer to God for our own actions. But I *am* bone of his bone and flesh of his flesh and there is that of my father in me which helps to make me what I am and which made it right to stand where he once stood. I felt a deep need to say that it was good to be back, for although I knew it for so little time, the place where you are born and where you first learn to respond to the beauty and wonder of the world is in a very real sense 'home'.

I needed to say that only at a surface level is life merely a chronological sequence of events. There are certain happenings – the sudden loss of a parent in childhood, the death of a child or a partner, the breakdown of a marriage – that because they are so traumatic and life-changing seem to exist in a different dimension of time and be always deeply part of you. Yet what really matters is not what happens in this unpredictable world, but *how* we respond, what we make of what we are given, whether we have learned something about how even the starkest tragedy can be a means of grace that we might never have come to in any other way.

One of the deepest of Christian insights is that even in the worst of events God is present and there are possibilities of redemption. That is part of the meaning of the Cross: that good can be brought out of evil; that new life can emerge from an event that seems utterly final and devastating. And I believe that we and the local body of Christ that is now my father's parish were saying to him: 'We shall never know *why* you did what you did, for that is known only to you and to God, but your desperate cry for help came out of so much unrecognised anguish of spirit that it demands not our judgment but our deep compassion.'

I also needed to say to my father that meditating on his action has taught me that none of us can ever really understand the heart of another human being, and none of us dare pass judgment on anyone else's life or death. That is God's prerogative, for he alone perfectly understands, and his judgment is always more than matched by his mercy. Those rare photographs I sometimes glance at merely catch my father's surface likeness: they tell us nothing of the secrets of the heart. Besides, those who find life too painful or too complex to bear may have had the dice loaded against them from the start, and none of us know whether we would have survived if we had been in their place.

What we do know is that the God who is our judge is also our saviour, and that in Jesus Christ all we need to know of God is once and for all defined. Defined in the only terms we can hope to understand. In terms of a man who shares our living and our dying; who loves the sinner and heals the sick; who waits on those he calls his friends and washes their feet; who seeks out and consoles the despairing; who describes the transcendent God as being like a father waiting and watching for his penitent child to come home; and who hangs on the Cross out of love for us.

The friend of whom I spoke just now has written this of his own father's death: 'God is present in such events not as their cause but as the one who even in the hardest of them offers us the possibility of that new life and healing which I believe is what salvation is … I cannot tell how God was present in my father's death … but my faith and my prayer is that he was and that he continues to be present with him in ways beyond my guessing.'

The possibility of new life. The certainty of healing. The power of 'the love that will not let me go'. Our eyes fixed not 'on the things that are seen, but on the things that are unseen'; for (as St Paul writes) 'what is seen is transient; what is unseen is eternal … No wonder we do not lose heart.'

The God revealed by Christ is not only our creator who knows our inmost hearts, but also our redeemer who, even as we turn to him in penitence, has forgiven us and welcomed us home. I do not believe my father needed me to tell him that. For I believe that when he fell to his death he was in the deepest sense caught and held in the everlasting arms of the one who is the merciful and loving Father of us all.

37

Final Eucharist as Dean of Westminster

29 NOVEMBER 1996

Westminster Abbey

The *Cambridge Evening News* had a certain inspired knack of producing memorable misprints, often by leaving the final consonant off a word. Reporting the farewell service of a local Pentecostal minister they once informed us that 'at the end a large crow remained in the church singing *Abide with me'*.

The great 17th century Master of Trinity, Cambridge, Isaac Barrow, who taught Isaac Newton, preached twice in the Abbey. His first sermon, he told Dean Sprat, had two parts to it: the first treated of slander, the second of lies. 'I beg you,' said the Dean, 'to confine yourself to slander,' which reluctantly he did, and preached for one-and-a-half hours. You would have thought they would have learned their lesson. But no, he was invited back and on this occasion, after Barrow had preached for a solid hour the Vergers called for the organ to be struck up and (I quote) 'he was blowed down'. Today my colleagues' fingers start drumming and their feet start tapping if a sermon at the Abbey Eucharist exceeds eight minutes; but tonight I crave your indulgence for just a touch longer.

My text may strike you as odd, even perverse: the words of the penitent thief to Jesus on the Cross: 'Lord, remember me when you come into your Kingdom'. And I seize on one word in particular: the word that seeks to catch the eye of everyone who enters the Abbey in daylight, for it dominates our striking new memorial to the Innocent Victims of war, oppression and violence. It is the word *'remember'*. At first sight that would seem to say no more than: 'don't forget'. But there is nothing simple about the word 'remember'; it is a word vibrant with meaning, a kind of theological carpet-bag of a word that, once you begin to unpack it, will lead you to the very heart of the Christian mystery. So let me try to do just that.

There is a sense in which tonight is about remembering. Remembering some of the events of these past ten years, great and small; remembering members of the Abbey Family whom we have loved and who have died; remembering friendships made, crises shared and surmounted; remembering Christmasses and Easters and the Abbey in all its moods. Remembering and being thankful, and saying to each other 'I won't forget you'.

And is there any other church in Christendom which has remembering so poignantly built into it? A remembering of the war dead focused on the grave of one unknown warrior; or in the forest of tiny poppy-bearing crosses that surround the Abbey and St Margaret's at Remembrancetide; or in the solemn bearing of the book to the High Altar on Battle of Britain Sunday; or in the need to come here for special services to commemorate eighty years since the Somme and Gallipoli, fifty years since El Alamein and Monte Cassino. And all this touches people's deepest need to remember those who have been an intimate part of their lives and always will be.

But what is this 'remembering' in the light of the mystery that is me and the paradox that we call time? For you and I hold together in our minds the memories of a life-time, so that our lives are both linear and instant. Here tonight, inside my head, I am all I have ever been: the six-year-old me, pining for a lost father, the thirty-something-year-old me falling in love, the fifty-year-old me over-stressed in a demanding parish, and the sixty-seven-year-old me on the eve of retirement. They all co-exist in this mystery called 'me'. And it is the same for you. The past and the present are one in the moment that is now. And it's because we are all we have ever been that we can recover, and as it were re-*member*, re-assemble, those we have loved and lost, putting them together again, bringing them out of the past and into the present.

I am claiming that this act of re-membering is much more than a not-forgetting. For its opposite is dis-membering. To dis-member is a destructive thing: it is to take apart a body limb by limb, to destroy it. To 're-member' is to do what 'all the king's horses and all the king's men' couldn't do to Humpty Dumpty: put him together again.

And so, when the penitent thief says to Jesus: 'Lord, *remember* me when you come into your Kingdom' I find much more in those words than just the negative 'don't forget me'. I hear him saying: 'Lord, re-member me, re-create me, put me together again, but this time in your own image and as you have always intended me to be.'

For in the end that is why we are here. Damaged, dislocated people, asking to be re-membered, re-created as the Body of Christ. We are those who recognize in Jesus Christ our true likeness, our proper humanity, the person God intends us to be, and our prayer is: 'Lord, re-member me, re-fashion me so that I may share the life of your Kingdom. Remake my life in the shape of your own.' And his answer? 'If you would truly re-member me, if you would bring me out of the past into your present, then *do this* with bread and wine.'

And in our imagination we watch him as he takes bread in his hands and offers it, thanks God for it, breaks it, shares it. Says: 'This is me – this is the pattern of my life. You now are to re-member me, that is to say, to be my body in the world, your lives offered to God, your lives lived thankfully, your lives broken and shared in the costly service of others.' And that is why every time we do this we are *re-membering* him, taking what lies in the past and making it present, making *him* present. But also we are saying: 'Lord, re-member *me*, re-create *me*, in this foretaste of your Kingdom. And that is why the Eucharist, like God himself, is both in time and beyond it. For in it we may look back at the past, to this man doing these actions; we may equally look to the future and see people coming together to break and to share bread (with all that means in our unjust world), people who are open to God and each other in his new creation we call the Kingdom. But chiefly we may glimpse here the God revealed in Christ who is to be met in each other now or not at all, here or nowhere; re-membered, embodied in us.

Deans and Canons and Minor Canons come and go, and congregations change with the passing years; but the Abbey abides. Yet it abides as no more than a beautiful but ultimately empty shell unless at the heart of it is a community of people who day-by-day, Sunday-by-Sunday, year in and year out, are embodying Christ, recalling into the present his life, his death and his Resurrection, their persisting desire that, however long it takes, they may be re-fashioned in his likeness. And re-membered when he comes into his Kingdom.

38

The Costly Way of Reconciliation

20 JULY 1997

Royal Chapel, Great Windsor Park

Some words from St Paul's letter to the Ephesians that were read as the second lesson: 'Pray also for me that I may boldly and freely make known the mystery' (in some translations the hidden purpose) 'of the gospel'.

This weekend some of us here are immersed in a conference taking place down the road at Cumberland Lodge. Its theme is *Preventing Future Wars*, with a sub-heading, *Commonwealth Strategies for Peace*. As you would expect, its main speakers have analysed the root causes of conflict in our world and how such conflicts may best be prevented and resolved; and they have focussed on the potential role of a unique grouping of countries: not the United Nations, but the Commonwealth.

Today many write off the Commonwealth as redundant in a world where, in terms of the economy, all the headlines are claimed by Europe, and in terms of defence, by NATO. What they choose to ignore is that quite other sorts of bonds and relationships can form the basis for effective and creative international bodies. The Commonwealth has emerged out of the stirring (if chequered and sometimes traumatic) history of Empire, and therefore its members are linked by powerful emotional bonds that lie deep in our common history. And the most significant thing about this Commonwealth of 52 nations is that it bridges some of the most intractable divisions of our world. What other grouping of nations contains such striking divisions of race and culture, of the First and the Third worlds, of great wealth and heart-breaking poverty?

The way the Commonwealth functions has been likened to a flock of migrating geese. When geese fly in formation they help each other, for as each goose flaps its wings it creates an uplift for the goose behind. Which means that geese flying together have a 70% greater flying range than would be the case if each bird was to fly alone. And if a goose begins to lag behind or fly out of formation, the others 'honk' it back into position. Currently the Commonwealth Heads of Government, after years of honking at South Africa, are honking at Nigeria and Sierra Leone, for at the very top of the Commonwealth's Charter, its Declaration of Principles, are a commitment to justice and human rights, and the establishment of that international peace and order which cannot exist where such rights are denied. And some of its most effective work has been done by the Secretary-General or his emissaries in attempts to prevent and resolve conflicts in Lesotho, in Papua New Guinea, in Kenya, in Fiji and in Bangladesh. And for this work the Government allots to the Commonwealth Secretariat what amounts to peanuts. How ironic that we should spend 22 billion pounds annually on defence, yet consider this particular work of peace-making and reconciliation within the nations of the Commonwealth only worth the paltry sum of some £100,000 a year.

Peace-making and reconciliation. Of all the great services in Westminster Abbey during the past decade, the one that is indelibly printed on my mind was the one held to welcome South Africa back into the Commonwealth, from which she had been forced to withdraw in 1961. The Abbey was packed to the doors. The 51 Commonwealth flags had been carried in procession up to the high altar by representatives each in their national dress and placed in grouped stands, leaving one empty space. At a certain point a young South African naval cadet arrived at the west door with the new flag which

153

he carried up the nave, to be met at the quire entrance by Vice President Mbeki, who took the flag to the altar steps where the Commonwealth Secretary General, Chief Anyouku, placed it in the empty stand. The entire congregation erupted into spontaneous and lengthy applause; a group from Soweto led us in the new national anthem; Bishop Trevor Huddleston led the prayers, and Archbishop Desmond Tutu began his sermon with what seemed the only appropriate word: 'Wow!' – and afterwards danced for joy on the steps of the Abbey. He danced because we had witnessed the most striking example any of us could remember of what St Paul calls 'the mystery of the gospel'. For that purpose is, in a word, *reconciliation*. Our reconciliation with God through Jesus Christ; and in turn, our reconciliation with each other. Both stem from a readiness to forgive and to be forgiven: to forgive and be forgiven the wrongs of the past and the present. And it is a 'hidden' gospel because it is in such stark contrast to our natural instinct, which is to retaliate when we are attacked or hurt or treated unjustly, to store up anger in our heart, to claim 'an eye for an eye, a life for a life'. And it is 'hidden', 'a mystery', therefore, because without a change of heart, we are blind to it.

It was not just Nelson Mandela who brought about a radical change in his nation by adopting the powerful way of forgiveness and reconciliation. It was Mr de Klerk who, a month after he had expressed deep apology in Cape Town for the evils of apartheid, gave the Nobel Laureate lecture in the Royal Albert Hall. When he had finished, he was asked by a questioner whether apartheid had been brought to an end by international sanctions? 'No,' de Klerk replied, 'it was not the sanctions, it was deep self-analysis on our knees before God'.

For what such deep analysis on our knees can reveal is a way of acting that is radically at odds with the way of the world. What has been hidden to us is now revealed, for we begin to see with new eyes, and with a new awareness of what the gospel is actually about. For there is a weak and impotent gospel, which sees Christianity in terms of a series of moral injunctions and Jesus as our example; but there is a powerful gospel, which has as its centre the Cross and Passion of Christ and which speaks of forgiveness and dying, of resurrection and new life. It speaks of a God made known in human terms, who says: 'Accept that you are loved. Accept that you are forgiven and reconciled. Then live in the light of this knowledge, and treat others as I have treated you.'

I am not so naif as to think that such a liberating truth can be easily translated into the way nations behave to other nations; or indeed that justice can be achieved and conflicts resolved without great cost. For it's justice that we are talking about. That is the ground-rule for all proper human relationships. Yet people's conflicting interests and desires can rarely be reconciled with absolute justice for all. Almost always there has to be compromise, and that inevitably means some sacrifice. All parties have to relinquish something which strict justice might have awarded them; and that, however modest, is an act of generosity – if you like, a small act of love.

It is also clear that past hurts and offences carry a powerful poisonous toxin that will frustrate every attempt to neutralise it unless and until there is a deep desire to pursue the costly way of reconciliation. You only have to think of Northern Ireland or of a longstanding family row. There has to be a facing of painful and bitter memories, and an attempt to look back and *understand* what happened, for it is only by understanding what has led to such a state of bitter hurt and anger that there can be any hope of mutual penitence and mutual forgiveness. You cannot forget, but you can forgive. Only then can the healing of those memories take place. In the words of T.S. Eliot: 'Only by accepting the past can we alter its meaning'. But that requires grace and courage of a high order.

I have spoken of large matters: of the prejudice, the past injustices, the conflicting desires, that divide nations and societies. But you will understand that I have therefore also been speaking of those destructive forces we all harbour within our own divided hearts. I began with South Africa and what two men achieved by following the alternative way of forgiveness and reconciliation. And I end with another man's visit some years earlier to that same land, and his very personal attempt to apply the powerful, hidden gospel of Jesus.

Roger Schutz, Prior of the ecumenical community of Taizé in Burgundy, was in Cape Town during the years when Nelson Mandela was still imprisoned on Robben Island. He visited a black neighbourhood and writes that night in his diary:

> I thought we should be meeting a few friends, but found a whole crowd gathered for prayer. African priests and pastors of all denominations welcomed me on a platform and handed me a microphone. I spoke some words to them ... but I said to myself that my words were so inadequate. So instead ... I tried to express all that was in my heart with a gesture. I said: 'I would like to ask your forgiveness, not in the name of the whites – I could not do that – but because you are suffering for the Gospel and you go before us into the Kingdom of God. I would like to pass from one to another of you so that each of you can make the sign of the cross on the palm of my hand, the sign of Christ's forgiveness.' This gesture was understood immediately. As I moved among them, each one made the sign of the cross on the palm of my hand. It seemed to take an eternity. And then, spontaneously, they burst into songs of resurrection.

39

A New Commandment

30 JULY 1989

Westminster Abbey

And Jesus said: 'I give you a new commandment.'

For six Sundays running during these Sundays after Pentecost the Gospel at the Eucharist is from St John. His is a Gospel which turns entirely upon the experience of loving and of being loved. Whether the author is John the beloved disciple or not, what cannot be denied is that the man who wrote this Gospel has grasped at the very centre of his being the overwhelming truth that he is loved. That God in the person of his Son has said to him: 'I love you because you are you.' And his whole Gospel is therefore a sustained reflection on what it means to be loved by God; and in turn to love others.

If you ask to me to define this love as we are both to experience it and express it, then I would say it is at the very least the recognition of the true value of each human being in all his or her uniqueness and singularity. It doesn't primarily have to do with feelings. It has to do with perception – how you see – and with behaviour. It has to do with how we act towards each other: in a word, with a desire to *serve* and be of service. That is why, where the other three Gospel writers see the climax of the Last Supper as Jesus sharing with his disciples the bread and wine of the Eucharist, St John tells instead of how on that last evening with them Jesus laid aside his coat, puts a towel round his waist, and begins to wash their feet. 'There!' says John. 'There you see what the majesty of God is like!' 'The Word was made flesh,' says John, 'and we beheld his glory.' And if you ask him 'when?' he replies: 'When we saw the Lord down on his knees washing our feet'. For here, in this humble act of service, is an image of the true meaning of love.

Here is the love seen in God's action in giving his Son for the world's salvation. The love which is seen at work in Jesus' action in seeking out men and women and drawing them into a loving relationship with himself and one another. The love which is defined in terms of living for others and – if need be – dying for them too.

So the fact that Jesus kneels before them as a servant tells them and us more about the true nature of God than a thousand sermons. God becomes man: that is an act of profound humility, the act of a God who makes himself vulnerable, a God who suffers. It is the act of a lover who will go to any lengths to capture the heart of the beloved.

And having shocked them at last into a glimmer of under-standing, Jesus says: 'Now I give you a new commandment: love one another as I have loved you. Because that is the only way people will recognize you are followers of mine.' Another way of putting this new commandment 'love one another as I have loved you' would be: 'go about your life *as those who are loved*'.

So what is new about this new commandment? What is new is that this love which is seen in serving the needs of others – this love that Jesus requires of his followers – is to be of the same kind with which he has loved and served us. He is describing the quality of life as God intends it to be: life in God's Kingdom of which the Church is to be the sign and of which life in our local Christian communities is to be a foretaste. And the more we know ourselves to be loved and valued by God in all our uniqueness and singularity the more we shall understand what it means for each local church to be a community of loving service.

When Jesus gave 'a new commandment' he was not speaking to the world, where all are enjoined to love God and love their neighbour. That is the old commandment and it remains valid. He was addressing his disciples, and he was speaking of the special bond of love which should unite all Christians: a love like that of Christ for each of us; a love which then spills over in service to the whole community. If we really were to go about our lives as those who are so loved, the power of the Church's witness would be irresistible. And out of that nucleus of self-giving love would flow the power to make others see what it means to love their neighbours as themselves.

I end with some words of Archbishop William Temple, which he first wrote exactly fifty years ago.

'The old commandment, "love your neighbour as yourself", stands as the universal, and universally neglected, requirement; the new commandment "that you love one another as I have loved you" has a narrower range and an intenser quality. When we Christians keep the new commandment, the world may keep the old.'

40

The Story of My Days

11 JULY 2002

I treasure the moment ten years ago when I sat with the new boys on the first Sunday of term at Westminster Abbey Choir School. The boy on my left was a wide-eyed 8 year-old. I tried throughout the meal to engage him in conversation, but he did not utter a word. He just listened and, as he ate, his eyes never left my face. Which can be quite disconcerting. Finally, just as the meal ended, he said somewhat dismissively: 'So, *basically*, you're the Dean of Westminster.'

But he was wrong. Basically I was *me*, the *me* I have been since the September day I was born in a Northamptonshire rectory and will be till the day I die. Basically I am, as you are, an integrated whole of body, mind and spirit; shaped by my upbringing and a lifetime of experiences both joyful and painful; one who was called upon to play for a while a succession of professional roles as faithfully as I knew how, but with a consistency and an integrity that has made me uniquely me, with a unique journey, and with an integrity which death will not undo but rather complete. Each one of us is called to be – and increasingly to become – our true self, nobody's role-model and nobody's clone.

On the eve of his execution in 1618, Sir Walter Raleigh, a prisoner in the gate-house prison at Westminster Abbey, wrote a poem on the theme of time,

> ... which takes in trust
> Our youth, our joys, and all we have,

160

And pays us but with age and dust;
Who in the dark and silent grave
When we have wandered all our ways
Shuts up the story of our days.

It is 'the story of (my) days', my own journey of faith, that
Rachel Maurice has encouraged me to speak about this morning: a journey through 70 years of the 20th century and
hopefully a good few of the 21st. Both the outer journey, and
infinitely more important, the inner one. The outer journey
can be fairly quickly despatched. My mother was a tennis
player (12 years at Wimbledon), my father a country rector
who, one Saturday afternoon when I was three, committed
suicide by throwing himself off his church tower, leaving my
mother both homeless and penniless. It was a strange, largely
wartime, childhood, lived in a series of rather seedy rented
rooms and boarding houses. I grew up, a somewhat lonely
only child, wanting to be an actor, but at school I was much
influenced by a charismatic headmaster, and other seeds were
sewn. I did my two years' National Service in the R.A.F.
alongside Ronnie Corbett, which was entertaining, and then
Cambridge alongside Peter Hall, which led to far too much
acting, and where I read, first English and then Theology. I
was trained at what is now Ripon College, Cuddesdon, served
a curacy in Hertfordshire, then became chaplain to the
Bishop of Southwark, Mervyn Stockwood, during the lively
60s in that animated diocese (where I learned more than I
ever wished to know about the workings of the Church of
England). I then got married and moved to a 15,000-strong,
largely council-estate parish with two curates and three
churches. After seven years I was appointed as Head of Religious Programmes for BBC Radio, and for seven years I
commuted to London and worked in the secular and
demanding context of Broadcasting House, seeking to reflect
on the four radio networks and also on BBC World Service the
spiritual life of this country, as well as Christian values and

beliefs. We did so in nearly 30 programmes a week, ranging from Choral Evensong through 'Thought for the Day' and the Daily Service to documentaries on Radios 3 and 4, a popular People's Service on Radio 2 (long since gone), and *Jimmy Savile's Speakeasy* on Radio 1.

From the BBC I moved to Cambridge to be Vicar of the University Church, Great St Mary's, seeking to bridge town and gown and meet the needs of large and very different congregations. It nearly killed me, and after six years' hard work I was housebound for a year with what was eventually diagnosed as ME (Myalgic Encephalomyelitis). In 1986 I was well enough to go to Westminster Abbey, which I served with great delight for ten years, retiring at the end of 1996 from a medieval deanery to a modest Victorian terrace house in Salisbury, where I write books, conduct retreats, do some counselling and spiritual direction, and learn pottery. Which, after a lifetime of using my brain and exploring the world of words, is wonderfully refreshing. All this has been a welcome return to anonymity and normality. And after a restive life it has felt more and more like coming home.

I've tried to bring together both my outer and inner journeys in a series of books: the experience of illness and recovery in *A Year Lost and Found*; the fruits of a sabbatical in letters to my grandchildren on the subject of wonder and the implications of giving proper attention to whoever or whatever lies before your eyes in *This Sunrise of Wonder*; a distilling of the rich ministry of a great church like Westminster Abbey in *Pray, Love, Remember*; and finally, last autumn, in a book called *Learning to Dance*, which is at once an endeavour to meet the Richard Dawkinses of this world with the affirmation that post-Darwin, post-quantum physics, post-modernism, you can still hold the orthodox Christian faith without being written off as a clown, and also an attempt to set out with honesty what it means to be human.

T.S. Eliot used to tell of getting into a London taxi one evening. 'You're T.S. Eliot,' said the driver. 'I've got an eye for a celebrity. Only the other evening I picked up Bertrand Russell and I said to him: "Well, Lord Russell, what's it all about?" And do you know, he couldn't tell me.' To be on the human journey is to be aware of what Eliot called 'the mystery of things'. The writer Philip Toynbee tells, in the journal he kept in the months before his death from cancer, of the priest on whose ministry Toynbee came to depend: '12 November 1981: This evening I asked John how he came to be a clergyman. He told me he had tried several things first – engineering and psychiatric nursing among them – but this was the first pool he had stepped into in which he couldn't feel the bottom. A wonderful answer.' There may be some unenviable people for whom life holds no mystery, but most of us are aware of what has been called 'a beyondness at the heart of things', aware that the whole is somewhat greater than the parts, aware of the transcendent – that which is greater and other than we are, and just out of reach. It is what artists strive to capture; it is what causes many scientists exploring the mystery of inter-stellar space or the human genome to speak of their sense of wonder.

If there is a connecting thread running through this talk it is my powerful belief, which has grown stronger with the years, that learning to become human is what it's all about. To believe in the incarnation, to believe that the Word takes flesh in Jesus, that matter is God's best and most effective language, is to have a passionate concern for the human. The journey of Jesus of Nazareth, from Christmas to Easter via Good Friday, not only provides us with a window into God: it also gives us the definitive view of what it is to be human. Yet so often we Christians clothe our insights into truth in the kind of exclusive language that only the enlightened will understand. But if our experience doesn't resonate with the common experience of humanity, then our words will be unheard. St Paul says that it is in God that every human being 'lives and moves and has their being', that each one is created in the image of God. Augustine and Eckhart and the author of

The Cloud of Unknowing and Teresa of Avila knew this, as did poets like Thomas Traherne and Hopkins: for them God not only pervades the whole universe, but is silently present in every human soul waiting to be recognised, and can be known directly by love by every human being who really desires to know him. 'God in all things: all things in God.' If this is so, then 'human' and 'Christian' don't describe different *kinds* of beings. All are called to become human in the truest and fullest way. In the words of St Irenaeus: 'The glory of God is a living person fully alive and the life of each living person is to see God.' Words which are echoed by the Orthodox priest, Fr Dimitru Staniloae, who writes: 'The glory to which humanity is called is that we should grow more and more God-like by becoming more and more human.' What Christians have to offer is simply a different frame of reference, one that by God's grace enables us to become what we truly are, to see with changed eyes, to look at God and the world and our neighbour and to perceive (to use Martin Buber's terms) that everything is a Thou and nothing is an It.

What I have to say tonight is the fruit of forty years of a mixed bag of a ministry, at the heart of which have been two compelling desires: *to be a useful pastor*, and *to retain my humanity*. All spiritual experience, all Christian belief and practice, is rooted in our common humanity. Sit and listen to anyone telling the story of their days, and you will find yourself listening to the common story that binds us all: a story that contains love and hurt and pain, loneliness and belonging, desire and disappointment, anger and guilt, the need to forgive and to be forgiven, that are implicit in the costly business of living and loving. Human beings are *this* sort of creature, searching, yearning, hungering, unfulfilled sorts of creature. The story of any one of us is also, in a profound sense, the story of us all. As Wordsworth wrote: 'We all share one human heart'. Humanity, it's been said, is like an enormous spider's web: touch it anywhere and you set the whole thing trembling. Which is why your story, your journey, awakens all kinds of echoes in me, and vice versa, and this recognition of the familiar is the beginning of that kind of sympathy we call compassion. When this happens, our loneliness has been met. A gulf has been bridged between one human being and another. I do not believe there is a lovelier word than 'pastor', nor a more important aspect of ministry than pastoral care; and I rejoice to be part of a church that recognises the right of every person in every parish to look to their clergy for care and affirmation in all the unpredictability of their daily lives.

Let me say a word about the role of the pastor. All public roles attract expectations as stones gather moss, and to serve as a deacon or priest, stipendiary, non-stipendiary or locally ordained, is to be the object of people's expectations. Those expectations will always exceed one's capacity to match them. They can weigh you down and cause us to run round our parishes, in the Psalmist's words, 'grinning like a dog', and wagging our tails ever more furiously. Some expectations are valid, some invalid, though it has taken me a lifetime to distinguish between them, and to learn that saying 'no' is as important as saying 'yes'. The two valid expectations are first, that we are there when anyone turns to us in need – just as Jesus broke away from the crowds to give his full attention to this or that individual; and second, that in the ordering of worship, in our use of words in preaching, in the conduct of the rites of passage, we shall be properly professional. Nothing matters more than the quality of our worship and the care and imagination we bring to arranging the space we have to fill. Simple, unfussy ceremonial matters. Worship that is ill-prepared and ill-conducted, or those who have lost any sense of wonder or the numinous in celebrating the eucharist or leading worship are, I believe, one of the commonest factors in emptying churches. We need constantly to ask, what is this space for? It is where we human beings, in all our marvellous diversity, may engage with the transcendent, and this space we have inherited is not any old space, but a holy space, the place where past generations have met in search of that encounter between the seen and the unseen, and which has witnessed their sorrows, their hopes and their joys.

But it isn't simply the outer space that should concern us, but the inner space that is to be nurtured and explored by those who are drawn to them: that inner space that Jeremy Taylor spoke of when he said that 'there should be in the soul halls of space, avenues of leisure and high porticoes of silence, where God waits'. The wit Sydney Smith said of Lord Macaulay that 'he talks too much, but he has occasional flashes of silence that make his conversation perfectly delightful'. And there is a sermon by Alan Ecclestone in which he says:

> The work of Christ consisted in his obedience to, his unswerving trust in, the Silence he called Father ....
> The world in which we live is a world in which God is silent. But it is filled with the Word of God – and it is for us who live by that Word to learn to listen to it in silence.

Nothing I did in my parishes seemed to me more important than the establishing of half-a-dozen simple contemplative prayer groups in people's homes, praying silently for the sick. At Great St Mary's I came to understand that the greatest need was to provide teaching on prayer, and also a contained space where people could be encouraged to sit or kneel in that simple giving of attention in which we practise the presence of God. So we transformed a side chapel, and gave it a visual focus, a sculpted figure of the risen Christ, and provided a number of prayer stools; and then set aside thirty minutes each day before Evensong for such a silence. And at Westminster Abbey its praying heart was not St Edward the Confessor's Shrine (though that was indeed a prayerful space), but St Faith's Chapel, tucked away behind a stout medieval door at the end of Poets' Corner, where every day started for those of us who ministered there just after 7 a.m. with a 20-minute corporate silence in a chapel whose air was heavy with the prayer of centuries, and where it was rare to drop in during the day and not find one or two people absorbing its stillness. Today in retirement, I still need the discipline of praying with others and I try to in Salisbury Cathedral's Trinity Chapel early most mornings. It is a wonderful space dominated by that great Prisoners of Conscience window standing above an Amnesty International candle, effectively linking prayer and action.

Looking back at my salad days, I would now question my motives for getting ordained, yet I have no doubt at all that I was meant to be a priest, and that nothing else could have fulfilled me to the same degree. Only this mysterious thing called 'ministry' in which men and women are called to be, in a phrase of Henri Nouwen, 'living reminders'. For that is what Jesus of Nazareth was: a living reminder of the true nature of God. 'What is the greatest problem you meet in the confessional?' a wise old Roman Catholic priest was asked recently. 'God,' he answered, 'people's false understanding of God.' Living reminders of what God has done in Christ: that he revealed in the only terms we can understand, human terms, to be Christlike, his name Father and his nature Love. In Jesus God is saying (as it were): 'I give you my Word, my Word made flesh, that you are loved with a love that cannot be broken. Trust me: I give you my Word.' And it is the whole body of Christ, ordained and lay, that is to be a living reminder to a forgetful world of the meaning of God's love in incarnation, cross and resurrection, even if some of us are as it were public reminders that our human stories are linked to that divine story that was told once in a birth, a life and a death like ours, in one who was vulnerable as we are and knows from the inside what it feels like to be human. And what it feels like is vulnerable. From first to last the journey of Jesus, like ours, was a journey in vulnerability. That is what incarnation implies: the readiness of God to be exposed to suffering, exposed in a world that can be dark and unpredictable, for love that is not costly is not love, and I have learned that people can draw strength from vulnerability if we will but do that most unEnglish of things and share it.

When I was first ordained, my incumbent, who was a deeply spiritual, but also a deeply vulnerable man – and therefore a very good pastor – said to me: 'As you stand beside someone, listening to their pain and need, you must have one foot in the river, but always keep one foot on the bank.' I knew what he meant, and I guess he was right. No counsellor will be of much help if both are floundering in deep waters, and you must be able to let go of people's problems when they have left you; but equally people are not problems to be solved, they are mysteries to be loved, and they will only be attracted to you in the first place if they sense or have learned that you are not afraid of sharing your own humanity. Let me take two personal examples. When I was convalescing from M.E. I wrote *A Year Lost and Found*. It was an honest book about what it felt like to be knocked flat in mid-journey and to know a certain amount of darkness. It was also about the sort of questions one should ask if the experience is not to be wasted and something creative comes out of what felt like a wholly negative experience. The response took me by storm; after fifteen years the book has sold 15,000 copies and is still selling, and I've found it hard to cope with the hundreds of letters that have come as a result and the many people who have come to see me. I now realise that it's because telling my story helped authenticate other people's stories, and that it has not mattered whether or not their own time of darkness has been M.E. or another illness, or a marriage breakdown, or bereavement. Professionalism so often involves a holding back of large parts of oneself, an avoidance of the vulnerability that can only enhance our priesthood if we know, and can show others, how to use it creatively and redemptively.

Second: I had never spoken about my father's suicide. In 1993 I had a letter from the then rector of my father's country parish saying that some of those who were children when he died and still remembered him would like there to be a memorial tablet to him. In those more judgmental days suicides had no memorial, so that his ashes were scattered to the four winds. So sixty years later I went back with my 94 year-old mother, my children and grandchildren, for the placing of a small named stone in the chancel wall. I stood in his pulpit and preached, and for me, for my mother and for the parish it felt a wonderfully healing experience. I was (as it were) reassuring that most vulnerable man whom I could not remember but whose genes I carry that we loved him. I tried to find words that echoed Hamlet's to his father's ghost: 'Rest, rest, perturbed spirit!'; but much more, words that spoke to that deepest of Christian insights: that even in the worst of events God is present and there are possibilities of redemption; that as with the cross of Christ, new life can emerge from an event that seems final and devastating. In the presence of the local body of Christ that was now my father's parish I was saying to him: 'None of us can ever really understand the heart of another. We shall never know why you acted as you did, for that is known only to God, but your desperate cry for help came out of so much unrecognised anguish of spirit that it demands not our judgment but our deep compassion.'

The following year I was invited to preach in a packed St Paul's Cathedral at the annual service for the Corporation of the Sons of the Clergy – a body that had helped my mother financially when he died. In St Paul's I simply told this story, and the sermon was then printed in *The Tablet*. Once again the response was moving. Scores of people spoke or wrote to me, many of them with a close loved one who had committed suicide, but who had never heard it publicly and personally addressed. I tell you this not to reveal things about which the British traditionally keep their lips sealed – as an elderly priest put it after reading *A Year Lost and Found*: 'Do you enjoy undressing in public?' – but because we do 'all have one human heart', and too often professionals (doctors, clergy, teachers) are tempted to let what they perceive to be the demands of their role overrule their humanity.

I want to end by paying tribute to a small handful of people (all now dead) who at various times have influenced my own ministry; and then add a post-script. They have been very different in temperament, but between them they taught me six great truths: *first*, that our only starting-point is a deep conviction that God, the awesome, unimaginable, creative power that undergirds the whole creation, has revealed himself as Christlike, and that in him (in Michael Ramsey's words) 'is no unChristlikeness at all'.

They taught me *second*, the implications of a truly incarnational faith. They taught me that the incarnation is a celebration of the human, that it breaks down that false distinction between sacred and secular; that (while utterly realistic about the nature of sin and the power of evil) the Easter people, should be constantly hopeful about human nature and the image of God to be found in it, undying optimists about the power of God's grace; that ours is a God-haunted world in which he is to be known and loved in and through all he has made.

They taught me *third*, that the Holy Spirit is as active outside the Church as he is within it, found in unexpected people and unlikely places; that it was the world and its life which God so loved and for which Jesus died; that the Church is but the agent for the Kingdom and that it is the Kingdom and its values that demands our loyalty.

They taught me *fourth*, the great virtue of forbearance, which I guess is a particularly Anglican virtue. It's a belief that the truth does not lie in this extreme or that extreme, not somewhere in the middle. It may lie, paradoxically in both extremes, which is why the Anglican way has been characterised by a refusal to condemn or to tread the easy way of partisanship, believing that no one person or party or tradition has a monopoly of the truth, and rejoicing in the very

170

diversity which may be enriching. They taught me to beware of that kind of narrow exclusivity which is at its heart judgmental.

They taught me *fifth*, the value of silence and the need for an inner space (though I was slow to learn the lesson); that what people need of their clergy most of all (in the midst of our busy lives) is stillness and the readiness to listen.

And they taught me *sixth* and last, that the eucharist, the holy communion, is the most perfect way of sharing in Christ's self-giving love: the way in which, as we take bread and wine, we bring the whole world under God's sovereignty. The way in which, as the bread is broken, we identify ourselves with his broken body; the way in which, as we kneel side by side at the communion rail, with all our faults and idiosyncrasies, we take our place in the holy community, the new creation, and have a tiny but true foretaste of life in the Kingdom of God.

And the post-script? If I was on that famous desert island with the choice of only one book (other than the Bible and Shakespeare), I would be tempted to take the Diaries of that most unusual Victorian clergyman Francis Kilvert. I love him for his humanity, for his wit, for his vulnerability, and for his pastoral heart. He would, I guess, be exactly the sort of person you would choose to have ministering to you when you were dying. And I love him because when he was asked why he had kept a daily diary during his short ministry (he died of peritonitis at the age of 39), he said it was 'because life seems to me such a curious and wonderful thing that it almost seems a pity that such a humble and uneventful life as mine should pass altogether away without some such record as this … It is,' he added, 'such a luxury to be alive'. Which echoes exactly my own prayer, during this last part of my earthly life, as I look back and around at the mystery. It is that I never lose my curiosity, my gratitude or my sense of wonder.